Daughter
of the Air

Daughter of the Air

The Brief Soaring Life

of Cornelia Fort

by Rob Simbeck

Atlantic Monthly Press

New York

Published simultaneously in Canada
Printed in the United States of America

FIRST EDITION

Library of Congress Cataloging-in-Publication Data

Simbeck, Rob.
   Daughter of the air : the brief soaring life of Cornelia Fort / by
Rob Simbeck.
      p.   cm.
   Includes bibliographical references and index.
   ISBN 0-87113-688-0
   1. Fort, Cornelia, 1919–1943.   2. World War, 1939–1945—Aerial
operations, American.   3. United States. Women's Auxiliary Ferrying
Squadron Biography.   4. World War, 1939–1945—Participation, Female.
5. Women air pilots—United States Biography.   I. Title.
D790.S539   1999
940.54'4973—dc21   99-22547
                                                            CIP

DESIGN BY LAURA HAMMOND HOUGH

Atlantic Monthly Press
841 Broadway
New York, NY 10003

99 00 01 02   10 9 8 7 6 5 4 3 2 1

To my parents,
Bob and Kathleen Simbeck,
and to all the WAFS and WASPS

Prologue

I t was a gorgeous Sunday morning, not yet eight o'clock, and Cornelia Fort was flying. She and a student pilot had risen from the runway of Honolulu's John Rodgers Airport into a brightening blue sky dotted with lazy fair-weather clouds. To the west lay Pearl Harbor and its crowded, still-sleeping naval base and, beyond that, fields of sugarcane. Past the industrial area to the north they could see forest and the Koolau Mountains. The Pacific rolled behind them to the south; to the east, toward a strengthening sun, were Waikiki, Diamond Head, and downtown Honolulu.

No one who knew Cornelia would have expected her to be anywhere but in the air on such a morning. Just twenty-two years old and a pilot for less than two years, she was already one of the nation's most experienced flyers. She had earned her commercial and instructor's licenses within a year and begun teaching, leaving behind her family's Nashville estate for a job in Fort Collins, Colorado. For two months now, since October 1941, she had been working at Honolulu's Andrew Flying Service.

Her student, a defense worker named Suomala, was practicing takeoffs and landings in an Interstate Cadet, a tiny two-seater owned by the flying service. Cornelia would later write about what happened next:

> Just prior to the last landing I was going to have him make
> before soloing, I looked casually around and saw a military plane

coming in from the sea. We were so used to military traffic and our respective safety zones that I merely noted his position subconsciously and nodded for my student to make his turn onto the base leg of the traffic pattern.

I then turned to look around to see if we were clear to make the last turn into the field and saw the other airplane coming directly toward me and at my altitude. I jerked the controls away from my student and jammed the throttle wide open to pull above the oncoming plane.

I remember a distinct feeling of annoyance that the Army plane had disrupted our traffic pattern and violated our safety zone. He passed so close under us that our celluloid windows rattled violently, and I looked down to see what kind of plane it was.

The painted red balls on the tops of the wings shone brightly in the sun. I looked again with complete and utter unbelief. Honolulu . . . was familiar with the emblem of the Rising Sun on passenger ships but not on airplanes.

I looked quickly at Pearl Harbor, and my spine tingled when I saw billowing black smoke. Still I thought hollowly it might be some kind of coincidence or maneuvers. It might be, it must be. For surely, dear God. . . .

Then I looked way up and saw formations of silver bombers riding in. I saw something detach itself from a plane and come glistening down. My eyes followed it down, down, and even with knowledge pounding in my mind, my heart turned over convulsively when the bomb exploded in the middle of the Harbor.

Most people wonder how they would react in a crisis; if the danger comes as suddenly as this did you don't have time to be frightened. I'm not brave, but I knew the air was not the place for our little baby airplane and I set about landing as quickly as ever I could. It was as if the attack was happening in a different time track, with no relation to me.

As Cornelia began her descent, she heard a brief burst of machine-gun fire and realized it was intended for her. She dropped the plane quickly toward the runway. As they touched down, Suomala broke their silence. "When am I going to solo?" he asked plaintively.

"Whether [he] knew what was happening or whether he was jesting, a possibility in which I found little humor, I don't know," Cornelia later wrote. "I don't recall whether my answer was the one later accredited to me in the newspapers—'Not today, brother'—but that summed up the situation as I saw it." She taxied toward the hangars.

"That the attack did have relation to me was brought forcibly to my attention a few seconds later when I saw a shadow pass over me and simultaneously saw bullets spattering all around me," Cornelia wrote. She and Suomala jumped from the Cadet and sprinted for cover. Bullets tore into the tiny plane behind them.

I was doubtless a little authoritative when I arrived at the hangar and said in a voice creaking with excitement, "The Japs are attacking," but I was unprepared for their disbelieving laughter and their dismissal of the whole thing as some sort of maneuvers. I didn't stop to think that they were trying to deny it as long as possible, a natural form of wishful thinking, but with the danger gone for me, at least momentarily, I suddenly reacted in anger. I was damn good and mad that they didn't believe me. Just as I was about to protest, a mechanic ran up from a lower hangar and said hoarsely, "That strafing plane that just flew over killed Bob Tyce." [Airport manager Tyce, flying in a Cub with a student, had landed hurriedly and was killed as he ran toward the hangars.] I looked at him in horror and my scalp prickled. I knew bullets aimed at me had killed a friend.

Suddenly that little wedge of sky above Hickam and Pearl Harbor was the busiest, fullest piece of sky I ever saw. . . . Our antiaircraft started belching shells which left their puffs of smoke scattered like so many umbrellas floating thru the air, planes darting in and out, high and low. One came screaming down in flames, leaving a crimson wake; the detonation of the bombs bursting shook the ground under us.

"I was sort of trembly inside," she told a reporter later, "and the ground was shaking all the time from explosions." Many of the scores of Zeros roaring by were no more than fifty feet off the ground. One, she said, had to turn quickly into a vertical position to get between two tall buildings. The first bombs dropped at Hickam Field fell on the Hawaiian Air Depot buildings and others down the hangar line, filling the air with thick smoke.

We counted anxiously as our little planes came flying home to roost. Two belonging to Bob Tyce's company never came back. They were washed ashore weeks later, on the windward side of the island, bullet-riddled. Not a pretty way for the brave little yellow Cubs and their pilots to go down to death.

Those of us on the Honolulu side were lucky. The enemy planes were hell-bent on Pearl Harbor and flicked only a few careless bullets at us en route.

We couldn't decide whether to put all the planes in the hangar and make one good target or whether to leave them out and open to general strafing (which never came as the enemy pilots weren't concerned with our little putt-putts when battleships and military planes were nearby). During the height of the attack we saw a bomber coming in very low, directly toward us, and deciding that the hangar was not a very smart place to stand, we scattered.

For me and for some of the others as we later compared notes, this was the most unpleasant sensation of the whole day. It also crossed some of our minds that possibly we were the first Americans to run from invaders on American soil. This dubious historical distinction I would rather have done without. Even when we recognized the bomber as it came nearer to be an American B-17 (one of those coming from the mainland on a routine delivery flight), the guilty feeling was still in my mouth.

The B-17 pilot, Cornelia said later, "was so confused and excited, he landed downwind and nosed over."

After the first attack subsided, we drove up to Ole Andrew (my employer's) house high in Nuuanu Valley. The sights and sounds of Honolulu were sprinkled directly below us. We saw what was left of the fleet go steaming to sea in search of Jap carriers; we saw what was left of our air strength go out on patrol, all too late.

Cornelia spent the rest of the day drinking coffee and listening to police calls on the radio. Finally, under blackout conditions, she went to bed.

"There was nothing else to do," she said later.

One

D r. Rufus Elijah Fort was not a man given to self-doubt. The square-jawed, steely-eyed squire of Nashville's sprawling Fortland Farm saw no reason to doubt himself, his accomplishments, or his opinions. The son of one of the region's most storied families and a success at both medicine and business, he had become the perfect picture of everything the post–Reconstruction South had hoped it could be. His was a world with dignity and calm self-assurance as its bedrock.

After his graduation from Vanderbilt University Medical School in 1894, he rose swiftly to prominence, becoming chief surgeon and superintendent of Nashville City Hospital by the time he was twenty-five. He founded and ran his own fifty-bed hospital, the Fort Infirmary, where many of the city's young doctors and nurses did their intern work. He served on the boards of several others and was soon named president of the Tennessee Board of Health. He was chief surgeon for the Tennessee Central Railroad, providing care in his own converted railroad car, and his articles were widely published in medical journals.

But it was in the insurance business that Rufus Fort made his real mark. In 1902, when he was barely thirty, he was one of five founders and initial stockholders of the National Life and Accident Insurance Company, which quickly grew into one of the nation's largest debit insurance firms. The firm sold its "penny policies" door-to-door in many cases, and Dr. Fort and his partners turned their $10,000 investment into a money machine of a company that was eventually worth hundreds of millions of dollars. In the process, they helped put Nashville on the financial map.

Dr. Fort inspired loyalty and respect in the hearts of many; people told and retold stories of the early days when he made house calls in his two-horse carriage, driven by a black man named Charles, sometimes performing operations on patients' kitchen tables. Tall and imposing, he could also inspire fear and awe in the hearts of others, from acquaintances at the ultra-exclusive Belle Meade Country Club to those who worked with and under him.

Dr. Fort had earned a reputation as something of an autocrat. He held a firm grip on life at Fortland, his 365-acre estate on the Cumberland River, four miles east of downtown Nashville. His black houseman, Epperson Bond, might relay his orders to the other servants or to the field hands, but there was never any doubt as to who was giving them. Epperson spoke for Dr. Fort, and Dr. Fort's word was law.

It was the same way with the Fort children, whose privileged existence was tempered by the steady diet of hard work their father demanded. In 1924, there were four of them: Rufus Jr., thirteen, tall, thin, and serious; Dudley, twelve, easygoing and athletic; Garth, ten, red-haired and affable; and Cornelia, five, already gangly and tomboyish. With her open smile and blue eyes peeking out from under an unruly mound of thick, curly, reddish-blond hair, Cornelia could soften her father, if only a little, in a way her brothers could not. Dr. Fort, who was then fifty-two, did not exactly dote on her—he didn't really dote on anyone then—but he did seem to be amused by her straightforward spirit.

From time to time Epperson, who doubled as chauffeur, would take Cornelia with him when he drove into Nashville to pick up Dr. Fort after work. Invariably, she would ask her father to stop at the drugstore to buy her a treat. When he declined, she could generally win him over by challenging his gruff reluctance with a sweet, "But that's what daddies are for, isn't it?"

From an early age, Cornelia saw Dr. Fort precisely as he wished to be seen—as provider and lawgiver. He made it a practice to listen to his children's opinions on any number of matters, but all decisions were his. It was that way with chores. It was that way with schooling. And, in the summer of 1924, it was that way with flying.

A quarter of the way into the new century, Dr. Fort had already passed solemn judgment on the airplane. He had built a life, a fortune, and a reputation on hard work and intelligent calculation. He was not one to trifle with a whimsical piece of machinery. He had not even learned to drive a car—Epperson did his driving for him—and he was not about to be tempted by this rickety airborne toy of the flyboy adventurers.

Aviation seemed the life-threatening pastime of dreamers and ne'er-do-wells; for proof, Dr. Fort could point to Jersey Ringel and his Flying Circus, whose appearance at the 1921 Tennessee State Fair had been widely publicized in and around Nashville.

Dr. Fort owned a thriving herd of Jersey cattle that regularly won blue ribbons at venues like the fair, which was a prime showcase for agricultural products of all kinds. And it was there, amid the preserves and quilts, the sideshows, barkers, and games, the band concerts, trapeze acts, jugglers, and clowns, the parades of Confederate and Spanish-American war veterans, the Tunnel of Love, the Ferris wheel and nickel merry-go-round, the cotton candy, hamburgers, and muscadine punch, that Ringel had left the grandstand gasping.

He took off from a nearby farm in the passenger seat of a Curtiss "Jenny." Officially the JN-4-D, the Jenny was a 90-horsepower World War I biplane that could be picked up cheaply after the war and was a mainstay of the profession—if, in the early twenties, you could call aviation a profession. More accurately, it was simply an excuse for a group of daredevils to thrill themselves and others until, as often as not, they were killed or crippled. They went from town to town performing loops and rolls and spins in planes constructed of wood, wire, and fabric and held together by sewing kits, hammers, and wishful thinking. These barnstormers alternately amazed and horrified the crowds that gathered to watch them. Astonishingly enough, though, the same crowds usually contained a few foolhardy souls willing to pay for the chance to be taken aloft. Dr. Fort knew that sort of fool existed, and he had no patience with fools.

Ringel teetered into sight standing on the tiny plane's top wing, which stretched maybe 30 feet from end to end. The Jenny, piloted by Billy Brock of Chattanooga, swept low past the grandstand, and then circled. Ringel, waving to the crowd and balancing himself—without a parachute—seemed to defy every God-given instinct he possessed. He walked to one end of the wing, hooked his knees around a wing-tip skid, and hung there, arms waving in the wind. In a moment, another Jenny flew into position just above the first, a rope ladder swinging from its landing gear. The crowd held its breath as Ringel, sure enough, grabbed the rope and pulled himself up onto the lower wing of the second plane, got his balance, and stood motionless, his arms grasping the wing above him, as the plane did a loop.

Finally, he climbed into the front seat as the plane gained altitude and then, after a moment's hesitation, fell slowly into a nosedive. The engine went silent and the plane plummeted toward the crowd, as thousands of people, not sure whether this was planned or not, wondered if they should scramble toward the exits. At the last possible moment the engine started and the plane roared to life, leveling off just over the heads of the crowd and soaring away. It was joined by the original Jenny, and the crowd, its collective heart stilled and restarted, cheered, watching as the planes headed back toward the field they'd come from, magical specks growing smaller and smaller in the afternoon sky.

This kind of thing did not amuse Dr. Fort. Like it or not, though, the Jersey Ringels of the world were aviation's ambassadors, the romantic drifters who were gradually making the airplane a part of the American spirit.

The barnstormers may not have been the only reason for Dr. Fort's aversion to airplanes. During World War I, he was chairman of the draft examining board, and it is likely he had seen Nashville boys coming back wounded or killed after crashes. As an insurance executive, he knew a foolish risk when he saw one. He decided that aviation would have no part in his sons' lives.

This had been the "war to end all wars," but there could always be another one, he reasoned. He already had planned for his sons to attend military school. If they were ever called to war, they would go as officers, not enlisted men. His boys would not be cannon fodder, and they certainly would not be daredevils dropping from the skies as their airplanes sputtered nose-down over battlefields. Forts did not do such things. Yet Dr. Fort suspected that aviation, still in its infancy, might turn into an even stronger temptation as it matured.

And so, one afternoon in the summer of 1924, Dr. Fort called his sons into his study at Fortland. As Rufus Jr., Dudley, and Garth lined up, Dr. Fort brought out the family Bible. "I want you boys to put your hands on this Bible," he said, "and promise me you will never fly." Solemnly, each of the boys did as instructed, putting his hand on the Bible and taking the oath.

Cornelia stood in the hallway just outside the door. Her father had seen no reason to involve her in this ceremony. Cornelia, after all, was only five, and it was ludicrous to think a southern girl of her station would ever think of riding in a plane, let alone piloting one.

Still, Cornelia was drawn to the doorway. She waited, wide-eyed, as her brothers, each in his turn, faced their father. She listened as they made their promises. And, standing silently, she took in every word.

Two

ortland was a little girl's paradise. It stretched for two full
miles along the Cumberland River, on whose bank Dr. Fort
installed a bathhouse and lifeguard. He allowed people from
the community to come and swim until one summer when one
of them drowned. Shelby Park, a huge tract adjacent to Fortland
and the river, had earlier been the site of a roller coaster, shooting
galleries, and weekend balloon ascensions and parachute drops,
but now it was simply a large and lovely preserve, a cool, shaded
buffer between Fortland and the city.

Fortland was a working farm, and its rich soil yielded great
quantities of oats, corn, and barley, sorghum, soybeans, and pole
beans. Cornelia's mother told her about its early days, when she
would hear the field workers—most of them black and many of
them parolees from the Tennessee State Prison, where Dr. Fort
began his career as the staff physician—singing as they led their
mules to the fields.

For Cornelia, the lawns and fields and her mother's huge gardens were the stuff of pure adventure. In a third-person auto-
biographical sketch she wrote in college, Cornelia recalled

> three husky, domineering brothers who bullied her and spoiled
> her, a stolid butterball pony named "Tarbaby" [whom] Cornelia
> thought she had trained to be a Wild West bronco, a pet lamb
> who literally did follow her to school one day, gentle-eyed cows,
> a pleasant river at the bottom of the rolling meadows, sweep-

ing acres of bluegrass, and a tremendous garden full of cape jasmine and honeysuckle. Like Ferdinand, Cornelia liked to sit under the trees for hours and smell the flowers. But she always took a book along.

If her brothers looked amiable enough she would enter their pony races and compete in all the trees in the front lawn for the title of Tarzan.

That fourteen-acre front lawn was also the site of games of tag or Cowboys and Indians, sometimes played on horseback. There were as many as fifty ponies, pleasure horses, and brood mares at any given time. Cornelia rode well from an early age and quickly became fearless and adventuresome. She also loved more leisurely rides around the estate with her mother, who rode side-saddle, and especially with her father.

While Cornelia didn't share her mother's knowledge of and appreciation for each species of flower, she basked in the overall peace and beauty of the place. She would watch flying squirrels float from the water tower to nearby trees in evening air bearing the scents of acres of flowers and tree blossoms. She would stop and listen to the bobwhites, the whippoorwills, and the owls as fireflies rose slowly, blinking in the dusk. Hot days meant swimming in the river, watermelons cooling in a basin of spring water, and perhaps ice cream scooped out of big circular cheese molds.

The farm's anchor, visually and emotionally, was the big house, which sat on a bluff high above the Cumberland. It was a grand antebellum showplace modeled on Robert E. Lee's ancestral home, Arlington. Dr. Fort had added north and south wings to the existing structure, as well as a grand front portico with six fluted Ionic columns. The main entrance led through a forty-foot hall to a doorway under a circular staircase notable for its grace and beauty even in an era of impressive houses. Almost baronial in its splendor, the first floor boasted fourteen-foot ceilings and held a collection of swords and a suit of armor. The walls were hung with paintings and large hunting prints, and the windows on both first and second floors featured exquisite wrought-iron grillwork. The sweeping drive ended at an iron gate set in a long stone fence. A magnificent walnut tree, its trunk fully seven feet in diameter, towered over the entrance to the estate.

While Dr. Fort held sway in Fortland's barns and stables, it was his wife, Louise Clark Fort, who reigned over its gardens and its twenty-four exquisitely furnished rooms. Fifteen years younger than her husband, Louise was the daughter of a divorced woman who had moved from St. Louis to Boston and become an integral part of Boston society. Louise was a twenty-year-old member of the Friday Sewing Circle and served as hostess at a surgical conference dinner, where she met Dr. Fort. He was thirty-five and seemed destined, like his four surviving siblings, to remain single. He looked up, saw the blond debutante, and, in a rare moment of unpredictability in a highly regimented life, found himself absolutely enchanted.

"You know," he told her, "I may just have to take you back to Tennessee with me." She was intrigued, and after a proper courtship and a Boston wedding, she did indeed accompany him to Nashville, leaving a string of brokenhearted former beaus in Boston.

Well-traveled and educated at Miss Porter's School and Briarcliff College, Louise won the hearts of Nashville's self-protective

New South aristocracy despite her northern upbringing and the Boston accent she never lost.

"To many," a Nashville reporter once wrote, "she is the epitome of what a Southern lady should be." Tall and charming, Louise carried herself with regal elegance, sailing into a room, friends said, "like a duchess."

Still, Nashville, though it called itself "The Athens of the South," was a far cry from Boston. A city of 110,000 people, it was an important intersection for major rail lines, but it remained a cultural backwater. Upon their arrival, Rufus and Louise lived briefly at the downtown Polk Apartments, where Rufus's spinster sister Lizzie also lived. Downtown Nashville was filthy, with more than its share of slums, bordellos, and drinking and gambling establishments. The air was gray with coal dust, and the streets, paved with rolled crushed stone, produced alternate quantities of dust and mud. It was not long before the Forts found the house and farm that would become their country estate.

The contrast with Boston must have been a great one for Louise. The road conditions were so dismal the family spent winters in a downtown apartment, and she would never forget the resulting inconvenience. "You won't believe it," she said, many years later, "but [Fortland] was so far out in the country and the roads were so bad that I had three punctures one day when I drove out there from town."

Cornelia was born on February 5, 1919, just weeks before 250,000 people danced in the streets of the city, greeting victorious troops returning from Europe. By that time, the Forts were firmly established in the upper ranks of Nashville society. Early in his career, Dr. Fort was a member of the Dinner Club, a highly select group of Nashvillians who staged elaborate dinners and dances every month during the social season. Later, he joined the Hermitage Club and was asked to join the boards of several banks and universities. Louise made a name for herself as one of Nashville's most gifted and dedicated amateur gardeners. She was a founder of the Garden Club of Nashville, an organization as much concerned with social connections as with horticulture. She spoke on conservation to groups statewide and became president of the Horticultural Society of Davidson County. During World War I, with Dr. Fort serving as chairman of the local examining board, Louise took charge of all Red Cross knitting in Nashville. Early on, they had become members of the highly restrictive, rigidly WASPish Belle Meade Country Club.

Dr. Fort was narrowing the scope of his professional life by the time his daughter was born. He left the Tennessee Central in 1916, and in 1920, at forty-eight, he sold the infirmary. His main concerns thereafter were the newly expanded medical department at National Life—he was the firm's vice president and medical director—and the operation of Fortland Farm, particularly its herd of Jersey cattle.

Dr. Fort did not allow drinking at Fortland. Nevertheless, the estate was the scene of frequent parties and lavish picnics for friends and business associates, and Louise's elegance, charm, and sophistication made her one of the city's most renowned hostesses. On sun-drenched afternoons, she gave teas on the lawn at Fortland, complete with servants carrying silver trays, ladies wearing lace dresses and wide hats, and a small orchestra playing Strauss waltzes.

The Forts could be gracious hosts, but Dr. Fort in particular had a well-earned reputation for stiffness. "I was treated beautifully," a friend of Cornelia's said of her visits to Fortland, "but in a very formal way. They were formal people, and Dr. Fort was especially so." That formality extended to the Forts' relationship as a couple. They tempered their affection for each other publicly, and Dr. Fort never shared with his wife the details of his business dealings. Still, he could be genuinely warm with his family and with those who worked with and for him. He took a keen interest in every aspect of the farm's operation, and he surrounded himself with people from whom he could learn the business. His dealings with them were generally cordial and marked by the respect he showed anyone he felt had earned it, regardless of social station. He would often walk or ride around the farm, talking with his foreman or workers, sometimes with Cornelia at his side, asking questions, and giving instructions. He learned especially well when it concerned the champion Jersey cattle he raised. When it came time to sell them, it was Dr. Fort who would painstakingly write out their descriptions in longhand at his desk for the notices in the cattle breeders' publications.

Mrs. Fort, constantly preoccupied with her steady round of committee meetings, tea parties, and charity drives, had little time for or interest in domestic pursuits. She busied herself with civic activities and in her gardens, with their rows of flowers a hundred feet long. "Mrs. Fort was not the kind of woman who baked cookies," recalled Cornelia's childhood friend Elizabeth Craig. "The cook baked the cookies."

The Fort boys might be allowed to run barefoot during the day, but at dinnertime they donned jackets and acted like the gentlemen they were expected to become. At table in the formal dining room with its bay window overlooking gardens, fields, and pastures, conversation ranged from family matters to politics and current events. Dr. Fort would ask his children for their opinions now and then, and they were expected to have something to say. On Sunday mornings, with their children perfectly starched and meticulously groomed, Rufus and Louise could be found at the downtown Christ Episcopal Church with much of Nashville society.

The Forts set high standards for themselves and were equally demanding in their dealings with their children. Dr. Fort's commitment to the no-nonsense Protestant work ethic was unshakable, and he made sure the ethic was instilled in his children. "My father taught us all how to work," Dudley commented, many years later. "He said he was going to teach us how to work when we didn't have to so we'd know how when we did." Dr. Fort would look into the boys' rooms every morning at seven, waking them with a gruff "Get up, boys." On winter mornings, they were expected to tend the fireplaces and, later, the coal furnace that replaced them. They had any number of chores around the house and farm and often stood in line with the other workers on summer mornings to receive their assignments from the foreman. They rode their ponies to carry water to the fields, where workers raised great clouds of dust with their threshing machines, and Rufus Jr. delivered milk throughout the city and drove a mule wagon to carry produce to Nashville's open markets as he grew older.

Dr. Fort insisted his children attend Ross Elementary School, a public school where they would learn to meet and get along with people from every circumstance. Ross was two miles from

Fortland, but only on the worst mornings was Epperson called upon to drive the children to school. Otherwise, they walked.

Only when a second daughter, Louise, was born in 1926, when Cornelia was seven, did Dr. Fort begin to soften. At fifty-four, with greatly scaled-back professional duties, he doted on Louise. Pretty and blond like her mother, she seemed not so much a daughter as a grandchild.

As Mrs. Fort's interests lay in gardening and in social and charitable endeavors, the Fortland kitchen was ruled by the family cook, Paralee. A tall, stout, regal woman born in the Sea Islands off the South Carolina coast, Paralee lived upstairs. She had no children of her own, but Cornelia would often follow at her heels trying to catch the music of the Gullah dialect—a curious mix of pidgin English and West African languages—she still spoke. Biscuits were "roll-roun,'" Cornelia's baby sister was "shishuh," and "nyamnyam" told Cornelia it was time to eat all the wonders Paralee was preparing. The language barrier meant that Paralee dealt always with Mrs. Fort, who made the effort to decipher her speech; Dr. Fort never understood a word she said.

That effort, though, was repaid many times by Paralee's cooking, which was legendary. In Nashville society, every hostess prided herself on her cook's beaten biscuits, which were served at breakfast with ham or bacon and eggs or chicken hash, at dinner along with pork chops and roast chicken, or at formal receptions, where they were topped with country ham and used as hors d'oeuvres. Paralee's beaten biscuits, which she rolled by hand, passing the stiff dough again and again through her biscuit "brake," were the envy of every lady in Mrs. Fort's circle. Paralee was universally acknowledged to be a treasure.

Nearly every ingredient she used, from the sweet Jersey cream, butter, and milk to the eggs, meat, vegetables, and fruit, came fresh from Fortland. Each winter, farm hands slaughtered seven or eight hogs and prepared pork cuts, made sausage, and hung country hams from the rafters of a smokehouse with eighteen-foot-high brick walls. Cornelia grew intoxicated with the tastes and textures and aromas in Paralee's kitchen, and for the rest of her life she would find dining a delightfully sensual experience.

If the kitchen was Paralee's, day-to-day dominion of the rest of Fortland rested with Epperson. Tall, thin, and aristocratic in bearing, Epperson Bond was born in Spring Hill, Tennessee, in January 1891 and moved to Nashville to live with an uncle. He graduated from the all-black Pearl High School with an education that included a thorough grounding in Latin. After a stint as a teller at Nashville's black-owned Citizens Bank, he worked for a while in an automobile plant in Michigan. Dr. Fort hired him just before Cornelia's birth. He was perhaps most visible around town as Dr. Fort's chauffeur, but that was only a small part of his job. With Dr. Fort fulfilling his responsibilities as a town father, it was Epperson who oversaw the estate's daily routine. He assisted Mrs. Fort in the garden and waited table in the dining room. He greeted guests and handled routine matters with the field hands. And often, when Cornelia or her brothers needed help with homework or wanted quick advice, they turned to Epperson.

They often forgot that Epperson Bond had a life of his own. He was twenty-seven when he came to Fortland, three years after his marriage, and he had a daughter who had been born a year before Cornelia and another born a few months afterward. And yet Epperson was there when the Fort children arose, even if it was before sunrise. Every morning, he took the streetcar as far as it would take him—the line ended at Shelby Park—and walked the short remaining distance to the farm.

He was a man who inspired decorum in the children and their friends by his very presence. "We wouldn't misbehave while he was around," a childhood friend said, adding, "He was the most dignified man you ever saw." Perhaps every bit as much as their parents, Epperson taught Rufus and Louise's children what it really meant to be a Fort.

It was a lesson whose historic underpinnings were reinforced regularly. Every year, near the July 14 birthday of ancestor Elias Fort III, the entire clan assembled for what amounted to a Fort family celebration. They had gathered this way since 1887 on the grounds of the Mint Springs Tavern, a sixteen-room summer place on the family homestead in Robertson County, forty miles northwest of Nashville. Each family brought the best its kitchen had to offer, which for Cornelia's family meant Paralee's fried chicken and beaten biscuits. Country ham and barbecue, chicken and potato salads, stuffed eggs, pies, cakes, watermelons, and homemade ice cream were laid out on long tables. Children and adults alike spent the day playing games, swimming, and rowing on the nearby Red River.

Late in the afternoon, Joel Battle Fort, a member of the Tennessee Legislature and a circuit lecturer for the Tobacco Growers Protective Association who was prized as the family's "silver-tongued orator," would deliver a formal address on some aspect of family history. The task of writing those speeches fell to Dr. Fort's oldest sister, Miss Lizzie, a tiny redhead with a zealot's passion for the family's colorful genealogy and heritage.

Lizzie Fort was ten when the Civil War ended, and she had not been willingly reconstructed. She was an active member of the United Daughters of the Confederacy as well as of the Daughters of the American Revolution. Fiercely independent, she lived in downtown Nashville at the Polk Apartments, in a fashionable red-brick building on the site of the home of President and Mrs. James K. Polk. On November 9, 1908, Miss Lizzie had been a witness to the shooting of Prohibitionist *Nashville Tennessean* editor Edward Ward Carmack, who was gunned down by antiprohibitionists Colonel Duncan Cooper and his son Robin outside her window. The killing was one of the most notorious incidents in Nashville history, and Miss Lizzie's role—she was quoted during the resulting trial, although she had most likely heard rather than seen the shooting itself—quickly became a piece of Fort legend.

For the family celebration of 1927, Miss Lizzie fashioned a tribute to the various women of the Fort clan. "My dear kinspeople," Joel Fort began, speaking in the afternoon air to scores of well-fed relatives, "today on the land of our forefathers for over a hundred years, we have gathered to celebrate the one hundred and ninety-seventh birthday of our Grandsire, Elias Fort III, who married Sarah Sugg. I know of no more fitting tribute to his memory than a sketch of his mother, his sister, his wife, his daughters, his daughters' daughters, and on down through the female line."

Cornelia was eight that year, and she listened as her father's cousin recounted the saga of Elias's daughter Catherine, who had struggled against a cruel stepmother, an unscrupulous woman who had even tried to cheat Catherine out of her family slaves. There were cautionary tales; one of Catherine's descendants "was unfortunate in letting her heart run away with her brains, and fell in love and married a drummer, a handsome, nice man, far beneath her in family." And there were stories of intrigue and adventure; Elias's granddaughter Sallie had married Colonel Joseph Terry, becoming half of "the handsomest couple in Southern Kentucky." Unfortunately, Joel continued, the dashing colonel had developed "quite a taste for gambling" and even dared to sell Sallie's favorite slave, her cherished lady's maid and the nurse of her four boys. "This was too much," Miss Lizzie's narrative explained. "In tears, Sallie went to her two brothers, Joe and Ben, and told of her trouble. Immediately, Colonel Terry received an invitation to be out of the state in so many hours. Being acquainted with said brothers-in-law, he accepted at once, went back to Elkton, Kentucky, and remained there—no divorce, just a riddance. Her [Negroes] were all gotten back."

These were the stories of a family that viewed itself in epic proportions. The Fort men were heroes and gentlemen. According to a cherished Fort legend, the entire family may have been descended from Robert La Forte, who had deflected a blow meant for William the Conqueror at the Battle of Hastings in 1066. They could with certainty trace the family to Huguenots who fled France for England in the face of Catholic persecution. Three Fort brothers—Moses, Arthur, and Elias—were part of a British force sent to Virginia to quell a 1676 uprising known as Bacon's Rebellion, and all three remained in the colonies, with Elias settling in North Carolina.

Elias's grandson, Elias III, served in the Revolutionary army, became sheriff of Edgecomb County, and served for forty years as a Baptist deacon. Then, in the fall of 1790, at the age of sixty, he led his family on an exodus of biblical proportions. With his nine children and their spouses, his grandchildren, and the family's slaves, Elias trekked through mountainous wilderness toward sparsely settled western territory. They came on horseback and in ox wagons loaded with household goods, leading their livestock to Fort Nashboro on the Cumberland River in what would become Nashville. They were forced to stay there through the worst of the winter weather until they could set out again for land granted by the state of North Carolina in partial payment for Fort's Revolutionary War service. He and his children and their descendants would own thousands of acres of adjoining land in the Red River Valley for well over a century. "From the marriage of Elias Fort, whose memory we celebrate today, to Sarah Sugg came a host of descendants who have contributed largely to the development of our State and Nation and who are yet prominent in the upward march of civilization," read Miss Lizzie's chronicle.

It was a saga with which Cornelia became amply familiar, even as a child; she understood how it led directly to her father and then to her and her brothers. Fortland itself stood just a few miles downriver from the spot where Elias and his family spent the winter of 1790–91. She also understood the special position she and her siblings held in the family. Dr. Fort was the youngest of ten children of Colonel Edmund Augustus Fort, who had purchased a large Robertson County estate in the mid-nineteenth century. Of the children who lived to adulthood, Rufus Fort was the only one to marry. His offspring were the last hope for his branch of the family.

Thus far, with five children of his own—three of them boys—
it looked as if Rufus was indeed fulfilling his role as preserver of
the Fort bloodline. And with his success as a doctor and business-
man, he was clearly doing his part to protect the family reputation. He took seriously the responsibility of making sure his sons
would add still more luster to the Fort lineage. He could have
had no idea it would be Cornelia, who sat listening on that July
afternoon to tales of women at the mercy of shiftless bounders,
who would lead the family into a new sort of adventure, more
daring and, in its way, more glamorous than even Miss Lizzie could
have imagined.

Three

The simple, idyllic days of Cornelia's childhood came to an end in the early 1930s. Her brothers were away at school or beginning their careers, and Cornelia made her inevitable entry into the highly formalized world of Nashville society just as her body began its adolescent changes. The carefree little girl now faced lace gowns, formal dances, and the social niceties designed to prepare her for the life her parents' position would give her. As she did, her genes betrayed her.

Both parents were tall, and by the time Cornelia was thirteen, she had shot up to her full height of 5 feet 10 inches. She was painfully aware of her size, although she would gamely insist, on a college application, "It used to make me self-conscious. Now I am glad I am tall." (Her sincerity can be gauged by the fact that she shaved an inch off her height on the application.) She had inherited her father's strong jaw and high forehead, features the upswept hairstyles of that era emphasized rather than softened. Her mother's natural grace and blond good looks had bypassed her, going instead to little Louise.

Cornelia had always been a tomboy, boisterous and competitive. As her teenage years approached, she might still find occasional release for such behavior around her brothers, but she knew that was not the way a young lady acted in Nashville society. Bookishness was no route to popularity either, but Cornelia was not about to give up her beloved reading. Isolated at Fortland, she devoured whatever she could get her hands on.

Since she had been ten or eleven, Cornelia had been carrying armloads of books home from the public library. She would spend her afternoons curled up in a bay window or lying on a sofa, Beethoven or Schubert on the record player, a dictionary at her side, looking up every word she didn't know. At ten she "adored" the Little Colonel books and devoured the reminiscences of Irina Skariatina, who had been a houseguest at Fortland. In her early teens, she developed a special fondness for Sir Walter Scott, James Fenimore Cooper, and Charles Dickens. "I like good biographies," she wrote. "I like stories of the sea, of pioneers, of social problems. I like anything but *True Confessions* murder stories."

Her brother Dudley was amazed by her ability to retain what she read. One afternoon he encountered her lying on the couch, turning pages almost too rapidly for belief.

"You cannot be reading that book so fast," he told her.

Cornelia took the challenge with cool self-assurance. "Pick out any page you want," she said, handing him the book. "Read me two lines, and I'll tell you the next one."

He did, and she did; the episode left Dudley astounded for the rest of his days.

Still, Cornelia knew better than to broadcast that side of her personality. A smart girl was likely to intimidate boys, and she was operating at enough of a disadvantage. "She was smarter than the rest of us, and I think most of us knew it," recalled her girlfriend Elizabeth Craig, "but she hid it all the time. Those little bumpy-faced boys didn't want to think she was smarter than they were, and she was just too tall and too big and too smart to be a flirt."

Otherwise intelligent and vivacious, Cornelia fell apart in the presence of the opposite sex. She later wrote, "I can carry on a conversation with almost anyone but prep school boys. I can feel at ease with babies, grandpas, debutantes, etc., but young boys terrify me."

The most painful times of all were the nights of dances. In the 1930s in Nashville, the social life of a well-to-do teenager was filled with dances, easily more than a dozen a year. Most were formal, with the boys in white tie, and many were held at the Belle Meade Country Club in the city's most exclusive neighborhood. One young Northerner who visited Nashville frequently during those years remembered the social scene, with its evident prosperity, its lavish displays of southern hospitality, and its inbred guest lists, as nothing less than "overwhelming." Cornelia, on the other hand, treasured as one of her favorite times a "small Sunday-night supper in midwinter where the few intimate friends sat around the fire and discussed all subjects, relaxed, ate apples, and acted naturally." For her, a crowded ballroom could be a place of unmitigated anguish.

A Belle Meade dance adhered to strict time-honored rules. The hostess, first of all, paired the couples for the evening. A girl might be asked if she had a preference regarding an escort, but often she was given no choice in the matter; the boy and the girl were simply told they would be attending the dance together. If for any reason the boy declined to take the girl with whom he was paired, he was expected to stay home.

Such occasions, after all, were not intended as "dates." The guest list nearly always included a core group of the same twenty or thirty young people, perhaps with a few out-of-towners, who might well be the excuse for the dance in the first place.

It was the boy's responsibility to pick up the girl, escort her to the party, which began no earlier than 9 P.M., and then take her home again, sometimes as late as two in the morning. At the dance, boys without dates formed a stag line. Throughout the evening, except during a few "no-break" numbers, they would cut in on dancing couples. As a result, the girl was expected to stay on the floor throughout the dance, with an occasional pause for refreshments. Ideally, she would dance with dozens of boys during the course of an evening. But it never seemed to work that way for Cornelia. A cousin, Miss "Hank" Fort, ran Fortnightly, a sort of private academy where the children of Nashville's upper crust learned to waltz and fox-trot; Cornelia was a poor dancer nonetheless. Her male friends would make sure she had an occasional change of partner, but it didn't happen often. If a boy brought her, he had to be prepared to stay with her throughout the evening.

From her very first dance, Cornelia loathed them all. Dudley remembered driving her to Elizabeth Craig's house on the evening of the first one, when she was thirteen. Cornelia became so nervous on the way that she began crying. Dudley did his best to calm and reassure her, telling her she was going to have a good time, but even he was not convinced. He felt, he said, like a mother taking a child to her first day of school.

She resented having to "fuss and carry on over makeup," Elizabeth said, "but she desperately wanted to be popular with boys, so she did the best she could." Her best, however, was never good enough.

The parents of some of Cornelia's friends offered solace, predicting she would simply be a late bloomer. "When Cornelia Fort is thirty," insisted the father of her friend Betty Rye, "she's going to be the most attractive woman in Nashville." Such predictions, though, were no consolation for a teenager. Hostesses were hard-pressed to find boys tall and good-natured enough to serve as escorts for her. Years later, Cornelia would remember these parties as "a seething mass of unfriendly souls" with nothing in common except "aching feet and a sense of heat and fatigue."

Cornelia had some relief from social pressures during her years at the relatively egalitarian Ross Elementary School, but even that escape valve was closed in high school. The Fort children attended private secondary schools, and Cornelia entered Ward-Belmont, the well-respected, very proper all-girls school attended by the young women from Nashville's "better" families. Located far across town from Fortland, Ward-Belmont had its genesis in the mid-nineteenth century as Ward Seminary, the alma mater of Cornelia's aunt, Miss Lizzie, who founded the Ward Alumni Association. The student body included the daughters of lawyers, bankers, and business executives and of families like the Cheeks, who had developed and marketed Maxwell House Coffee, and Atlanta's Candlers, who had made a fortune popularizing Coca-Cola.

Girls attended classes amid the splendors of Belmont mansion, with its vaulted ceilings, grand staircase, and Corinthian columns. This, however, was not just a finishing school; Ward-Belmont had earned a reputation for strong academics. A good percentage of the teachers had master's degrees or doctorates, and there were outstanding programs in art, interior design, and music. The sports program was rigorous; there was a swimming pool, and the school had a huge riding park and stables where students could board their own horses. Discipline and dress codes were strict, and there was much talk about religion and patriotism. More than two-thirds of Ward-Belmont graduates went on to higher education. Still, the school's ultimate aim was to prepare young women to marry and take their places in society.

Cornelia entered Ward-Belmont in 1932, with the nation in the depths of the Depression. Some Nashville businessmen had certainly been affected by the stock market crash in 1929. Most notably, the financial empire of banker Rogers Caldwell had fallen apart, forcing the closing of 120 banks in seven states. Caldwell's partner, newspaper man and financier Colonel Luke Lea, a key developer of the exclusive Belle Meade subdivision, had landed in jail. There had been a handful of suicides among the business elite. On the streets of Nashville, there were soup lines and panhandlers, peanut vendors and strawberry sellers. There was a shantytown on the banks of the Cumberland. While many businesses and individuals foundered, National Life flourished, selling its version of security in the midst of despair. Advertisements on its own 50,000-watt radio station, WSM, helped the company's assets grow from $29.6 million to nearly $55 million between 1930 and 1937. Ward-Belmont pupils were certainly aware the Depression existed—President and Mrs. Roosevelt ate breakfast at the school during a tour in 1934—but for most Belle Meade teenagers, Ward-Belmont was a privileged enclave, and the parties and formal dances continued.

Cornelia, Elizabeth, Betty Rye, and their friends were an integral part of those activities from the beginning. In eighth grade, when most Ward-Belmont girls would have been asked to join a high school sorority, they chose instead to form their own. They called it SAP—the initials came from a monogram on a suitcase in the *Little Orphan Annie* comic strip—and their first party was a decidedly makeshift affair. They pooled their allowances, made cookies and punch, hired a piano player (whom they paid with a $10 pair of evening gloves), and held the event at Fortland. Before long, SAP parties had all the predictable Belle Meade trappings, with boys in white tie and a full-scale orchestra for dancing, and the presence of a socially powerful SAP contingent became a necessity at parties hosted by the leading local fraternities. The fact that Cornelia was quickly part of the most prestigious girls' club in town did nothing to make the events any easier for her.

In Cornelia's crowd, every activity was a group activity. Even if a couple managed a single date for a movie, they usually wound up at a party of twenty or thirty boys and girls, dancing and eating at one of their houses. "There was something going on all the time," recalled a frequent northern visitor to Nashville. "We'd go horseback riding at Fortland, then go to a fancy lunch at the Belle Meade Country Club, and there would be all these dances. A couple of the boys had cars with rumble seats. They lived it up, and we had a great deal of fun, without doing anything bad." Cornelia may have hated the large formal events, but she could be more herself in the informal gatherings popular with her crowd.

Sometimes Cornelia's girlfriends spent much of the weekend at Fortland. They might take an afternoon trip into Nashville for a movie and shopping—the girls had signing privileges at the better stores on Church Street. After the movie there might be an ice-cream soda at Candyland, a legendary wood-paneled ice-cream shop on Church Street. Then the girls would return to Fortland for dinner, Mrs. Fort all charm and elegance at one end of the table and Dr. Fort all rigid solemnity at the other.

On some occasions, the girls might head back to town for a recital or concert at the Ryman Auditorium. Later, the Ryman would gain international fame as the home of the Grand Ole Opry, but in the 1930s it was a major stop on the nationwide tours of all manner of theatrical troupes, dance companies, and classical musicians. It was there that Cornelia developed a taste for dashing baritones like Lawrence Tibbett and Nelson Eddy, both of whom also had motion picture careers.

Cornelia was capable of the occasional schoolgirl prank—bored with a frog-dissection demonstration, she and a friend once crawled out a window, returning later before the biology teacher, a Miss French, even missed them—but she continued to be a profoundly private young woman, someone who could easily withdraw, particularly in the face of arguments or unpleasantness. It was a trait people often misread for aloofness or haughtiness, and it was something she would never lose.

When Cornelia arrived home from Ward-Belmont in the afternoon, chauffeured as usual by Epperson, the grand house could be a lonely place. Her brothers were hardly boys anymore, and the games of Tarzan or Cowboys and Indians had long since given way to reading. She still adored Garth, but she was becoming more ambivalent about Dudley, an eccentric whom friends were already describing as "a bird." Garth and Dudley were still at college, and Rufus Jr. had graduated and joined National Life. He cherished his chances for conversations with Cornelia during his visits to Fortland, but they had little time together unless it was carefully scheduled. Louise, who idolized her older sister, was still a child.

As always, Cornelia continued to lose herself in books. With time on her hands and no nearby girlfriends to distract her, she read nearly every afternoon until dinner. She also kept a diary, turning to it regularly to give shape to her day-to-day thoughts. She joined the campus literary society, the Penstaff Club, and was generally acknowledged to be developing as a fine writer. Still, her friends and teachers came to recognize that Cornelia did well only when she wanted to, and even then she didn't always push herself. She would often dash off a writing assignment in half an hour that her classmates had struggled with all weekend.

On school mornings, as Epperson, in his chauffeur's cap, drove her across town to Ward-Belmont, he would watch in the rearview mirror as she sat in the back seat, engrossed in a book. "I could drive Miss Cornelia anywhere at all," he would tell friends, "and she would not know the difference." Now and then they would chat about her schoolwork, and Epperson, his fondness for Latin undiminished, would quiz her on its grammar and definitions.

It was help she sorely needed. Cornelia was an indifferent student when the subject didn't interest her, and Latin, math, and science all fell into that category. She particularly hated physical education. Two afternoons a week, Ward-Belmont girls were required to stay late at school for some sort of sports activity. Although Cornelia was an accomplished horsewoman and played a fair game of tennis, the physical training sessions became her bête noire. They also became a means of pushing tentatively against the boundaries of her closely circumscribed world. The excuses she made up for skipping phys ed were part of her first tentative steps toward rebellion and self-assertion.

Cornelia, never a top student, left Ward-Belmont ranked twenty-seventh in a class of fifty-six. As her senior year ended, she had little sense of her future. She toyed with the idea of becoming an interior decorator but questioned whether she had the "originality" to make a go of any sort of artistic career. Her father's domineering ways had left her with little confidence in her own decision-making abilities. In fact, some of her early efforts at breaking away from convention had backfired dramatically. When she was fourteen, Cornelia smoked a cigarette at Rufus Jr.'s wedding reception and Dudley caught her. It was a foolish display of adolescent rebellion, but Dudley, after waxing moralistic for a while, promised not to tell their parents. The promise scarcely lasted through the weekend. On Monday, Mrs. Fort confronted her. Cornelia, who cited "honesty, loyalty, and tolerance" as qualities she found most desirable in friends, was furious with her brother.

Dudley took the tirade in stride. A few years later, though, he made sure Cornelia's own words came back to haunt her. By that time Cornelia was smoking regularly, although always on the sly. One night at the family dinner table, as she held forth once again about the cherished virtue of honesty, Dudley could stand it no longer. "Cornelia," he said, "if you're so fond of this honesty, have you told your parents that you're smoking?"

The room fell silent. After a cavernous pause, Dr. Fort asked solemnly, "Daughter, are you smoking?"

Cornelia didn't speak to Dudley for a year.

However much her rebellion could backfire, Cornelia ached for more independence. She had spent much of her adolescence taking part in social rituals she disliked and hiding her intelligence from boys. More and more, she was beginning to realize the limits of her environment. "While I love wholeheartedly my family, my friends, my home and city," she wrote, "I want to gain a new perspective. . . . I want to see new faces, gain a new outlook on life. I think it will do me good to stand on my own feet."

She saw what seemed the perfect opportunity when she was asked to join a group of her Ward-Belmont friends on an extended tour of Europe. The scrupulously chaperoned trip was intended to immerse the girls in the culture and language of each place they visited. They would, for example, read French history and literature and then visit the places they had read about.

Cornelia had traveled each August with her mother and siblings to visit family in the White Mountains of New Hampshire, and she had visited relatives or gone away to camp on occasion, but she had never been abroad or undertaken a trip of this magnitude. She wanted desperately to go.

Dr. Fort refused to consider it. Heartbroken, Cornelia turned to Elizabeth, whose grandfather, Cornelius Craig, was Dr. Fort's business partner and contemporary. Mr. Craig proclaimed the senior Fort an "old goat" and promised to intercede on Cornelia's behalf. "Don't you worry about it," he told Elizabeth. "When I get through with Rufus, Cornelia will get to go on her trip."

"Well, it didn't work," Elizabeth recalled many years later. "Grandfather came back to me and said, 'I did everything I could. Dr. Fort said he had never been to Europe, and there wasn't any point in thinking she could go to Europe either.'"

It is unlikely that Dr. Fort, aging and in increasingly poor health, and Cornelia, restless and hungry to break away, understood each other. On the other hand, Cornelia hardly understood herself. She seemed fully capable of self-delusion. In a college application, written around the time of her disappointment over the European tour, she insisted that the only problem of any weight I have ever had to decide was whether to go to college, if so, where, or to go to Europe for the winter or make my debut. My family left this entirely up to me because they want the results of my decision to be upon my shoulders. They wanted me to be happy.

She may have believed those words when she wrote them. At the very least, she was attempting to make sense of the only world she knew.

Four

ornelia had watched as the time came for her brothers to attend college; for each, the process was the same. Dr. Fort simply announced, at the appropriate time, that Rufus Jr., Dudley, and then Garth would attend Virginia Military Institute. Personal preference was not a part of the equation. VMI, in Lexington, Virginia, was everything Dr. Fort thought a college should be. The sons of other prominent Nashville families might go on to the Ivy League schools of the Northeast, particularly to Princeton, which was favored by southern families. VMI, though, promised strict academic and personal discipline and maintained at least a facade of the egalitarianism Dr. Fort had sought for his children in public grade schools. It had the added advantage, particularly to a man who watched his accounts closely, of costing considerably less than the Ivy League schools.

Rufus and Garth took to the VMI environment readily enough. Young Rufus, in particular, liked the fact that, once the cadets were in uniform, "You didn't know if a man was worth a dollar or a million dollars." He became active in ROTC and taught at the school for a year before returning to Nashville to work for National Life. The free-spirited Dudley was another story. His first year was an academic disaster, and he learned quickly that he was not cut out for military drills. The turning point came on a winter night when he was assigned to guard duty in the midst of a blizzard. Later, he recalled pacing back and forth in the flying snow, telling himself over and over, "My father didn't mean for me to do this." Undoubtedly, such rigors were exactly what Dr. Fort *had* wanted for the least serious-minded of his sons. Still, given Dudley's miserable grades and his dislike of VMI, Dr. Fort was finally convinced that his own alma mater, the University of the South at Sewanee, Tennessee, might be an acceptable alternative, and he allowed Dudley to transfer there. Sewanee's academic standards proved no more lenient than VMI's, though, and Dudley eventually abandoned college altogether, taking a job as a National Life branch manager in Atlanta.

When her time came to plan for college, Cornelia must have known she was headed for yet another confrontation with her father. She dreamed of going to Sarah Lawrence in the New York suburb of Bronxville. Cornelia had heard much about the college from her New England relatives, and she had girlfriends who had gone to Seven Sisters schools, but in following their lead she had selected the very sort of institution Dr. Fort dreaded most.

The school's faculty included geniuses-in-the-making like Martha Graham, Joseph Campbell, and William Schuman, all working under the guidance of Constance Warren, a champion of progressive education who outlined her then-radical ideas in the book *A New Design for Women's Education,* which appeared in 1940. Warren knew her approach could frighten people. "No marks, no lectures, no recitations, no exams, no textbooks," she wrote. "No wonder it sounds like a country club to many who know nothing about modern education but these spectacular half-truths." She demanded that students be "treated as individuals with minds and ideas of their own, no longer as children supposed to do as they were told, on faith."

Dr. Fort, of course, was convinced Cornelia needed "the guidance and discipline necessary to the proper building of character in any girl of her age." Warren, meanwhile, decreed that each student had within her "the seeds of what she is capable of becoming" and that the faculty's job was to "set her free for the adventure of learning." There were no required courses and relatively few restrictions on the students' behavior. There was a midnight curfew, but the young women monitored the comings and goings at their own dorms. Following a pattern loosely based on the British university system, each student was expected to establish a working relationship with a don, a faculty member who served as mentor, academic counselor, and, to some extent, personal adviser throughout her college career.

To make matters worse, Sarah Lawrence was one of the nation's most expensive colleges for women. Tuition and housing, which came complete with maid service, ran to $1,700 a year, a figure that did not include day-to-day living expenses or evening and weekend outings, of which there would be plenty, given Bronxville's proximity to New York City.

Dr. Fort would have none of it. He had chosen for Cornelia the all-female Ogontz School and Junior College. True, Ogontz was across the Mason-Dixon line, in Philadelphia, but it was rigorous and structured, and it had something no other women's college offered: military drilling. Carrying dummy wooden rifles, the women of Ogontz regularly took part in close-order parade-ground drills. It was essentially a continuation of Ward-Belmont with the addition of VMI's rigors. To Dr. Fort, it seemed perfect. As he had with his boys, he decreed that Cornelia would attend Ogontz.

Cornelia, for whom simple physical education was a chore at Ward-Belmont, dreaded the prospect of Ogontz. She resigned herself to at least one year at the junior college, but she did not go silently. She begged her father for the opportunity to apply to Sarah Lawrence for her sophomore year, that of 1937–38.

Perhaps convinced Cornelia would make her peace with Ogontz, Dr. Fort allowed her to complete the Sarah Lawrence application. Asked about her future academic plans, she demurred. "I don't know definitely," Cornelia wrote. Still, she could not escape her frustration at the trip her father denied her. "I plan to travel as much as possible, perhaps to take special courses at some university or foreign school. I plan to make my debut and eventually marry." Still, it was precisely the kind of vague conventionality from which Sarah Lawrence hoped to liberate its students.

Cornelia disliked Ogontz's gray walls from the first moment she saw them, in the fall of 1936. The school's most celebrated student, she learned, had been Amelia Earhart, who attended twenty years earlier and had since become an aviator, known around the world and second only to Charles Lindbergh in popularity. Just a year and a half earlier, she had made the first-ever flight from Hawaii to California. Cornelia was later fond of saying she was sure Earhart had taken up flying to escape the clutch of those "great gray walls."

Cornelia took some solace in the cultural life of Philadelphia. There, she had ready access to concerts by the Philadelphia Orchestra under its autocratic musical director Leopold Stokowski, who was sharing the podium that year with Eugene Ormandy, his eventual successor. In the 1936–37 season alone, the Philadelphia's guest artists included one of Cornelia's favorite artists, baritone

Lawrence Tibbett, as well as pianists Sergei Rachmaninoff, Artur Schnabel, Josef Hofmann, and Rudolf Serkin; cellist Gregor Piatigorsky; and the consummate Wagnerian duo of Lauritz Melchior and Kirsten Flagstad. On some concert evenings Cornelia was even joined by Elizabeth Craig, who was finishing high school at the Shipley School in Bryn Mawr.

Once she had settled in, Cornelia made the best of her situation. She impressed her teachers, as she had at Ward-Belmont, with her abilities as a reader and a writer. Her grades in English were solid, and she finished the year in the upper quarter of her class. At the same time, she threw herself into extracurricular activities, acting in three plays—her height made her a shoo-in for male roles in both *Little Women* and *Much Ado About Nothing*—and joining the equestrian team.

Still, Cornelia was just biding her time, and in February she updated her Sarah Lawrence application. Principal Abby Sutherland joined Dr. Fort in lobbying for Cornelia to stay at Ogontz, but back at Fortland, Mrs. Fort weighed in on her older daughter's behalf. She reminded her husband that she herself was a product of eastern schools, a fact that had not stopped her from becoming the model of a distinguished southern matron.

Late in the spring semester, Sarah Lawrence sent word that Cornelia had been accepted for the coming year. That acceptance came with a caveat; there was no guarantee her credits from Ogontz would be approved for transfer. Cornelia, surely, did not care, and with her mother taking her side, Dr. Fort at last relented. Cornelia could go to New York. For once, at least, patience and sheer determination had won Cornelia a victory in the face of her father's opposition.

Cornelia threw herself back into the Nashville social whirl that summer, riding, dancing, and playing bridge with her high school friends. There was one departure from that world, and it was a sign of how deeply Cornelia was still the daughter of Fortland. Just weeks before she set out for Sarah Lawrence, she applied to join Nashville's Chapter No. 1 of the United Daughters of the Confederacy. Miss Lizzie, still a major presence in the Fort family's life and a living link with the Civil War, had been a member of the chapter since 1896; she sponsored Cornelia's membership.

When the school year got under way, Cornelia found herself an unclassified student, neither a freshman nor a sophomore. If all went well, she would receive full credit for her Ogontz work the following spring, and her four-year Sarah Lawrence degree would be finished in three years. If her performance did not impress the faculty, her year at Ogontz would count for nothing, academically.

None of that mattered for now, as Cornelia was at last where she wanted to be. The campus, with its lawns and arbors, was picture-book Seven Sisters, snuggled amid oak, maple, and pine trees in a quiet residential neighborhood. Cornelia was exhilarated, jumping eagerly into its rhythms. During her first week on campus, she took personality, vocational, and values tests. Then, with the help of a temporary faculty adviser, she selected exploratory courses intended to acclimate her to the Sarah Lawrence experience.

The course load represented as big a challenge as Cornelia had ever tackled. Two literature courses involved extensive reading, from Flaubert and Balzac to Thornton Wilder and Virginia Woolf, with a number of required papers. One, Contemporary English and American Literature, was taught by her don, Maxwell Geismar, a twenty-eight-year-old Columbia-educated professor of literature with radical social and literary inclinations. He would establish a nationwide reputation four years later with the publication of *Writers in Crisis: The American Novel 1925–1940*. A psychology overview included field trips to New York's Children's Court for a study of child custody cases, a paper on the problems of southern blacks, and a major project on delinquency.

It quickly became clear, though, that Cornelia had no intention of becoming an academic drudge. Plunging into dorm life, she made friends with several of the girls on her floor—Sally Lowengart and Emylu Adams, both from San Francisco; Ann Perdue of Mobile, Alabama; and Rosalie Bangs of Providence, Rhode Island—girls from backgrounds like Cornelia's who shared a taste for tweed skirts, Brooks Brothers sweater sets, and pearls for everyday wear. Before long they were calling her "Cornie" and staying up until the wee hours, gossiping about men, classes, and the limited opportunities for on-campus social life over bacon-and-tomato sandwiches and milkshakes from nearby Gallatin's drugstore.

They played tennis, rode horses, and, as winter approached, took an occasional weekend ski trip. It was just a short walk down the Kimball Avenue hill to Palmer Avenue, past the shops and restaurants that led to Station Plaza, where it was easy to catch a train for the thirty-minute 35-cent ride to Grand Central Station.

Many of those downtown trips were class-related. In her literature class, for instance, Cornelia was assigned a paper on "Eating Out." The research included having dinner at the Bronxville Caterer and in Manhattan at Schrafft's and the Café Royal. More often than not, though, the girls needed no such excuse. One of the girls would take a $6 room at the Madison Hotel, and the others would come to "visit" and stay the night. "Three of us would sleep across the two beds," Sally recalled, "one would sleep in the bathtub, and another in a chair with an ottoman."

Cornelia, who had long bemoaned Nashville's lack of galleries and museums, thrived in New York. Her friend Helen Dixon's family had a Wednesday night subscription to the Metropolitan Opera, and four or five times a year she and Cornelia were allowed to use the tickets. The outings were glamorous by any standard. Helen's father would put the girls up at the Plaza Hotel. They would spend the day window-shopping, eating lunch at Schrafft's, and returning to the Plaza's Oak Room for dinner, which Helen signed for. Then, after the opera, the two girls would lie in their beds and chat. There would be small talk but they would discuss larger issues, too: Edward VIII had abdicated his throne less than a year earlier, the Nazis were on the rise, and Europe was becoming increasingly militarized. Helen, who traveled to Europe every year, had seen it all first-hand, but she found that Cornelia, whose hoped-for trip to Europe had been scuttled by her father, had no trouble keeping up with the conversation. "She was an intellectual," Helen said. "Really, she had a very good mind." What's more, trips to Manhattan gave Cornelia a chance "to get out of that sort of southern belle routine." Both in the city and on campus, Helen recalled, "Cornelia liked asserting her own personality and being her own boss."

Such cultural stimulation was a valuable part of the Sarah Lawrence atmosphere, but it wasn't long before it was taking its toll. Cornelia was often tired in class, and her teachers were not as impressed with her omnivorous reading as her teachers in Nashville and at Ogontz had been. Cornelia "has to stop reading so much and so fast and begin thinking a good deal more," Geismar said in his first report. She had too much "faith in the 'classics,'" he said, and she had been trained in "superficial and conventional forms." Cornelia was clearly in over her head when she was introduced to the work of Zola and of Korean poet Younghill Kang, and she dropped the psychology course and replaced it with William Schuman's Freshman Arts class.

By semester's end, Geismar could offer only faint praise for Cornelia's efforts. "She is willing to take criticism," he wrote, adding that "she is very much in earnest about her work." He acknowledged that the semester had been a "transitional period" and "a very difficult one for Fort." In just a few months, he recognized, "almost all her values have been questioned."

When Cornelia returned home for the Christmas holidays, however, it was not her own values she seemed to be questioning. Rather than share the difficulties she was having, she chose to act like the budding radical her father had always feared she would become at a Yankee school. "Daddy," she announced one evening at dinner, "my professor said the people who own radio stations and insurance companies are bloodsuckers." In case Dr. Fort didn't get the point, Cornelia added, "And that's how we've made our money!"

When a Sarah Lawrence freshman returned home after her first semester on campus, Constance Warren would caution, her parents could expect to find her in "the early stages of intolerance for what seems to her the hopeless conservatism of her family, her father's inflexible stand on politics, her mother's anxiety over her venturing alone in the subway. She may be pretty obnoxious that first Christmas vacation, airing her opinions and baiting her long-suffering parents." When it came to Cornelia, at least, Warren had hit a bull's-eye.

Five

S chuman's Freshman Arts class turned out to be everything Cornelia hoped it would be. Suddenly the music that had played in the background at Fortland while she read as a girl came to life as she learned to analyze major works by Brahms, Bach, Beethoven, and Tchaikovsky. The field trips included *Carmen* and *Lohengrin* at the Met, concerts at Carnegie Hall with Toscanini on the podium and Yehudi Menuhin as violin soloist, and performances on Broadway of *Our Town, The Seagull, A Doll's House,* and *You Can't Take It with You.* The semester's guest lecturers included Aaron Copland and Martha Graham. Cornelia threw herself wholeheartedly into the course, and Schuman decreed she had done work of "superior quality," praising her for her "seriousness of purpose and keen intelligence."

As a matter of fact, things were looking up in all of Cornelia's classes. That did not mean she was cutting back on her social life. On the contrary, as Cornelia became more comfortable with her Sarah Lawrence friends, there were more and more weekend trips to Princeton, Yale, and West Point. The excuse for the trip might be a football game, crew races, or a dress parade, but its real focus was the accompanying social whirl. This was far headier stuff than Cornelia had ever experienced in Nashville. She did not take to the party circuit naturally—she was still not much of a dancer—but she swiftly learned to enjoy herself in this rarefied atmosphere. Somehow, she did not mind huge social occasions when nearly everyone qualified as an outsider.

There was also the fact that these were, after all, college events, and some were decidedly lowbrow. While there were rigidly formal occasions like the West Point dances, at which each girl's dance card was filled out for her in advance, there were also occasions where the alcohol flowed freely, dance cards were unnecessary, and the social pressures were relaxed. "We were all heavy drinkers," said Cornelia's friend Sally Lowengart, "especially when we went to the men's colleges. It was considered very stylish."

The heaviest drinking, though, was the province of the men. At "house parties" sponsored by clubs and fraternities, it was not uncommon to see young men passed out on chairs and couches in the common rooms. Some, in fact, deliberately set out to drink until they passed out, sometimes several times in one night. It would not have been particularly rare, on such evenings, to see a young man totter toward the bathroom or outside to throw up.

There might also be a sloppy make-out session in progress, although there were clear, inviolable sexual boundaries. A good deal of passionate necking might go on here and there, but young women of Cornelia's acquaintance did not part with their virginity before marriage. If they did misbehave, they did not talk about it, and "sexpots" simply were not tolerated. Sally remembered the firestorm of gossip that blazed through their Sarah Lawrence dorm because of a girl down the hall "who, it was rumored, had slept with a man—that's how innocent we were."

This was life with a flair Cornelia found invigorating, and the alcohol helped her get past what remained of her nervousness. At the same time, she could not escape the cautiousness instilled by her no-nonsense, eminently practical father. When she borrowed a fox jacket from her Sarah Lawrence friend Rosalie Bangs for a weekend trip, Cornelia took out an insurance policy on it, Rosalie said, "just in case."

In fact, this was a time when Cornelia was finally able to draw somewhat closer to her father even as she exercised her freedom from him more fully. When she got to Sarah Lawrence, Dr. Fort would write an occasional letter, filled with news from home and fatherly advice. Without the bristling that often accompanied their face-to-face dealings, Cornelia was able to relax and react more calmly to what he said. She was now of two minds about her father. While she reveled in her ability to set her own course and establish her own rules, she also basked in the warmth and sense of family love he conveyed by mail.

Between trips and midweek overnights to New York City, Cornelia was tackling a heavy academic load as best she could and working as a staff writer for the Sarah Lawrence newspaper, *The Campus*.

Cornelia and her friends capped their year of social events with a mid-April boat trip to Bermuda, where they sunned on the beach, rode bicycles around the island, and flirted with the college boys there for the Easter holiday. Cornelia, in fact, fell for a Harvard student she met there, only to find herself disappointed when he began dating one of her friends.

Cornelia maintained a precarious balance between academics and extracurricular activities, but Geismar was convinced by year's end that she was adjusting "to a new environment which contradicts everything she has known in the past. This is in itself not a mean achievement." He was determined that she return "for another year, at least." On June 6, the school notified Cornelia that she would be permitted to return as a sophomore for the 1938–39 academic year. Still, she would not yet be given credit for her work at Ogontz.

Cornelia herself had begun to waver. The year had worn on her, and she began to doubt whether she even wanted to go back for a second. When she did resolve to do so, she found she had to persuade her father all over again. Her less-than-steady academic performance and his continued distrust of the school had combined to steel him against spending money for another unproductive year.

Geismar wrote to Dr. Fort, asking him to reconsider, and adding, "I have never felt either that [teaching her] was a loss of my time or that she would not be able to develop into an important person." Family members say that one of Cornelia's teachers showed up on the steps of Fortland and vowed to stay until Dr. Fort gave in. Eventually, he relented, although he laid down a corollary edict: Louise would never follow Cornelia to Sarah Lawrence. (Louise did, in fact, attend Sarah Lawrence after Dr. Fort's death).

Back home for the summer, Cornelia gave little hint that life in Bronxville had ever been a struggle. She seemed happy and newly self-assured. She even took the bold step of traveling to San Francisco to visit Sally Lowengart and Emylu Adams. Dr. Fort could not have been thrilled at the prospect, particularly when he learned that the young women had taken in a performance of the *Folies Bergère*.

As her second year at Sarah Lawrence got under way, Cornelia took her interest in the growing European crisis into the classroom. A course on European Politics gave her the opportunity to study the Continent's political dynamics and such works as Hitler's *Mein Kampf.* The syllabus could hardly have been more relevant. Germany had annexed Austria in March, and sanctions against Jews were growing harsher.

Cornelia also took a creative writing class that used an opening study of Hemingway, Faulkner, Lawrence, Steinbeck, and others to help teach structure and style. For a class on Thomas Mann, her teacher was Joseph Campbell, who would later achieve wide recognition for his study of myths and archetypes. Early on, he had difficulty sizing up Cornelia. "I cannot yet decide," he said, "whether she is really assimilating the materials which she greets with so much enthusiasm."

As the semester progressed, Geismar noted improvements in both her work habits and her temperament, but cited her "tendency towards generalized and hence vague work. This is in fact more than a tendency; it is with Cornelia something of a passion."

That vagueness was testimony to Cornelia's unwillingness to take a stand. For all her attempts to break free of her father's overwhelming presence, and for all her bristling at overbearing teachers, she found it difficult to function intellectually without their guidance. The same was not true of her views politically. In her second year on the staff of *The Campus,* Cornelia became chief editorial writer, and she was eager to flex her writing skills. Her views may well have been influenced by the unrelentingly liberal mood of the campus; every woman was expected to have a social conscience, and the students were urged to get out into the community and investigate social problems. Every Thursday night the dining hall served a pared-down menu so that money could be saved and sent to the Abraham Lincoln Battalion, a group of Americans, many of them students and Communists, who served on the Republican side in the Spanish Civil War.

Dr. Fort had long instilled in Cornelia, in word if not always in deed, the value of every person and the unimportance of social standing in determining his or her true worth. Still, she went far beyond her father in applying those democratic ideals. For instance, Sally Lowengart, from the beginning one of Cornelia's closest Sarah Lawrence friends, was Jewish. That fact was of no consequence at Sarah Lawrence, but it was noteworthy in the South. Sally once came to visit Cornelia at Fortland, and it is said that Dr. Fort did not want to allow the visit.

Anti-Semitism existed to some extent throughout southern society—no Jew had ever been a member of the Belle Meade Country Club—but Sally had not expected prejudice. Then, late one night, she and Cornelia and some friends were riding down a Tennessee highway after a party when Sally, riding in the rumble seat, spotted a roadhouse with a neon sign that read NO NIGGERS OR JEWS. "After that," she recalled, "I could feel the anti-Semitism in the air."

Hitler's increasing attacks on Jews in Germany horrified Cornelia. She was disgusted as well with the September 30, 1938, Munich agreement, which permitted German annexation of the Sudetenland. British Prime Minister Neville Chamberlain, who had proposed the conference that led to the agreement, was hailed by a British public thankful that war had been staved off, but Cornelia was having none of it. In her lead editorial for October 10, she wrote that Chamberlain is paving the road to world chaos. While Europe cheered his efforts for peace, now that there is time to consider that peace, the people of Europe are shamed. . . .

Better to go to war than lose the things that make life worth living. Germany was in no position to carry on an extended war. If the great powers had presented a unanimous front against Hitler and had been ready to go to a war that of financial necessity would have been brief, then the imminent danger of world Fascism would have been negligible. As it is Fascism gains prestige on the lips of every man able to read the paper.

Chamberlain has obtained peace but it is a disgraceful victory.

On November 21, shortly after Kristallnacht, which saw Nazis loot and burn synagogues and Jewish stores and houses in Germany and Austria, Cornelia turned her attention to the plight of the Jews in a piece headed "Barbarism à la Hitler":

Five years of barbarism reached its climax last week in Germany. After a five years' "purge," it remained for a minor incident to precipitate a wave of horror unparalleled since the Middle Ages.

Hitler announced his aim, that of purging Germany of all Jews, when he became dictator. How violently and horribly he has carried out his aim is all too apparent to everyone able to read. . . .

The tortures and human injustices that he has heaped on the defenseless minority is reminiscent of the Inquisitions and the early Christian Martyrs.

But surely this campaign of horror will turn on its creator and smash him also. Surely this wave of barbarism will weaken the ranks of Fascism and restore the faculty of healthy criticism to the mobs blinded with enthusiasm. We should aid the persecuted Jews with one hand and try to hasten retribution with the other.

Six

uring the 1938 Christmas break, Cornelia and her college friends gathered in Nashville for a dizzying round of parties, luncheons, and dinners. Capping it all was Cornelia's December 29 debutante ball, which *The Nashville Tennessean* called "one of the outstanding social events of the season." Nashville society gathered at the elaborately decorated Belle Meade Country Club, the best orchestra in town played, and Cornelia wore a décolleté gown of white illusion and silver embroidered lace. The only trouble was she didn't want to be there.

It wasn't that she hadn't warmed somewhat to such occasions. College life had given her a modicum of confidence and a greater ability to enjoy social events. Still, the full-scale theater of a debut—with her as its centerpiece—made her uncomfortable. It may have been that the club reminded her of the most painful moments of her high school years. "I don't think it was rebellion so much as that she just hated to be spotlighted," said her friend Helen Dixon. "She was a realist, and I think she thought it was superficial. She didn't like ostentation." Whatever the reason, Cornelia was not thrilled with the prospect of this rite of passage.

The debutante ball, though, was a firmly established tradition among Nashville's social elite, and Mrs. Fort stood on tradition and ritual, from the simplest afternoon tea to the most elaborate gala. And so, according to family legend, Cornelia was bribed into attending her own debut. Though no one remembers the booty, it convinced Cornelia to go through with the event because her mother wanted her to.

Classmates and acquaintances of both Cornelia and her long-time friend Elizabeth, whose debut preceded Cornelia's by two days, had gathered in great numbers for the events. Many of the city's grand houses, including Fortland and Elizabeth's home, teemed with male and female houseguests from eastern schools. Cornelia's Sarah Lawrence friends—Emylu Adams, Ann Perdue, Sally Lowengart, and Rosalie Bangs—all came. Governor-elect Prentice Cooper, a single forty-four-year-old, called Elizabeth's father, his old friend and Vanderbilt classmate, to ask if he couldn't escort one of the out-of-towners.

"The parties started the minute we got home from college," said Elizabeth, "and they were day and night and day and night." Not even the night between the two debut parties, held Tuesday and Thursday, was quiet. On Wednesday evening, 130 of their friends gathered at the club for dinner and dancing.

December 29 was crisp and cold in Nashville as men in tails and women in formal gowns entered the club, which sported elaborate floral decorations representing the four seasons. To the strains of a string quartet, the family received guests in the music room, decorated with smilax, peach blossoms, and pink tulips. Gift bouquets covered the grand piano and mantel. Many of the 400 guests—the governor-elect among them—had also sent gifts, ranging from evening bags to rare books, to Fortland beforehand. Rufus Jr. and his wife, Agnes, were joined in the receiving line by Dudley and his wife, Pearl; Miss Lizzie; Cornelia; and Mrs. Fort, who wore a black velvet gown trimmed in Russian ermine. Dr. Fort, who had been suffering from vertigo and was more and more confined to Fortland, did not attend.

At ten o'clock, the Francis Craig Orchestra, the city's most popular big band, struck its opening notes in a winter-themed ballroom. Cornelia, carrying a wrist corsage of orchids the florist replaced every twenty minutes or so, was led on to the floor by her brother Rufus for the first dance, and the ball was on.

Older guests watched from chairs that lined the perimeter of the ballroom as the younger set danced to everything from Strauss waltzes to current hits by Benny Goodman and the Dorseys. For quick breaks, they slipped into the canvas-enclosed terrace, which had been converted into a formal garden, for punch. At midnight, the orchestra took a break while the guests headed for an elaborate buffet supper in the music room, and then dancing continued until 2 A.M.

Every man was expected to dance with Cornelia, giving her the chance to chat briefly with all of them; there would be no time for uncomfortable lapses in the conversation. Friends said Cornelia found herself enjoying the party despite her misgivings, and the evening went much better than she had expected.

After the ball, Cornelia and many of her guests went back to Fortland for a late gathering. Her Nashville friends had seen little of Cornelia in months, and this was their chance to catch up and meet her new friends. The big house reverberated with laughter and conversation until dawn.

It was not easy, after all that, for Cornelia to begin studying again. Her socializing, which Geismar had once viewed as preferable to a lonely maladjustment to college, had become a stumbling block. He recognized that what she lacked was maturity.

She was an intelligent young woman who was nevertheless adrift. "Until she finds her true direction," Geismar wrote, "her present abilities will not be really fruitful. . . . She can do good work; she is likely to be sloppy about jobs when she's not interested in them, and overambitious when she is. . . . She needs mostly sympathy. She will work hard when she feels she's getting it, and like the spoiled little girl she sometimes is, will sulk and grow sad when she doesn't."

On June 10, 1939, Cornelia received her diploma as a two-year graduate. She was told her Ogontz work would not be credited, and she was accepted for return to Sarah Lawrence as a junior. She did not go back.

For a young woman of Cornelia's background, the future was laid out clearly, as if it were a country club ball. Social clubs, dances, the right dates, and an eventual marriage and position in Nashville society—that was the path Cornelia, under her mother's watchful eye, was expected to travel. Primarily to keep Mrs. Fort happy, Cornelia began to follow it. She and Elizabeth became two of about a dozen new members of the Girls' Cotillion Club, a mainstay of young society which held two formal and highly visible parties annually. Cornelia also joined the Junior League and an elite literary society known as the Query Club.

She continued to ride horses with Dudley, who had become an excellent horseman, or with friends like Fortland foreman Charles Kinle, who marveled at the abandon she could bring to riding and jumping. "She would ride anything in this world," he said. "She was wild, and what I mean by that is she just got a lot out of life."

Her brothers, who hunted regularly both on and off the grounds of Fortland, taught her to shoot, and Dudley introduced her to foxhunting, which she took to immediately. She seemed to be attracted as much to the toddies and warm fireplace chats as to the riding and hunting, and she would occasionally visit friends in other cities, making a weekend of foxhunting and socializing.

The following Christmas, more of Cornelia's friends made their debuts, and the elaborate round of parties and luncheons and dinners began again. In January, Cornelia was Governor Prentice Cooper's date at a dinner he hosted at the gubernatorial mansion during the Southern Governors' Conference. A month later, the governor attended a dinner party she hosted at the Belle Meade Country Club. Cornelia brought a new confidence to such events. There was no more hiding her intellect; she felt able and eager to discuss world events with an adult crowd. She was slimmer, she was dating, and the city's social life was active and glamorous.

Even so, it didn't take her long to realize that it wasn't enough. Twenty-one and out of college for a year, she was restless; her life had no focal point. Cornelia longed for travel, for excitement, for the kind of release a full gallop on a good horse could bring for a few moments. There was not enough on the Nashville social scene to hold her attention, and there was no new endeavor that could really fire her passion. At bottom, she hungered for a sense of direction that had thus far eluded her.

Seven

Cornelia might well have continued to drift, enjoying Nashville's social life as best she could, if not for two events in the winter of 1940. The first was Dr. Fort's admission to Vanderbilt Hospital. He continued to suffer from vertigo, and he was subject to attacks of angina. His symptoms worsened, and the family knew the end was near. As much as she had chafed at her father's restrictions over the years, Cornelia loved him deeply. The second came about as a matter of chance, and it took place, a family story holds, even as her father lay dying.

Cornelia and her friend Betty Rye were simply looking for a way to spend an afternoon. Betty's boyfriend, Jack Caldwell, was part owner of the Miller Flying Service at Berry Field, Nashville's newly opened airport, and Betty and Cornelia decided they'd give flying a try.

Each went up in a two-seater, Cornelia with Jack and Betty with Miller's chief pilot and flight instructor, Aubrey Blackburne. Cornelia, who knew nothing about airplanes, was completely unprepared for what happened next. At the moment the air caught the plane's wings and lifted it from the runway, she was transformed. The ground fell away, and she experienced a sense of freedom and exhilaration unlike any she had ever known. The plane rose and swayed and turned, and the trees and cars and roads and buildings shrank below her. As she watched the clouds come closer, Cornelia was both gleeful child and enthralled young woman. She had never felt anything more magical.

"She ate it up like it was jelly," Jack recalled. "She got up and didn't want to go back." They circled the area for just ten minutes, but the sight of the Cumberland River winding beneath them, the residential lawns, the wooded beauty of Mt. Olivet Cemetery and Shelby Park, and Fortland, with its cattle grazing along the river and the big house white in the afternoon sun, awakened something in her. When they landed, Cornelia jumped out of the plane.

"Oh, Betty!" she gasped. "If we wait a couple of hours, we can take our first lesson!"

Betty, who was decidedly less than thrilled by her own time aloft, fixed her with a firm stare. "Cornelia," she said, "if I never see Jack Caldwell again, I'm not getting back in another airplane."

Yet she listened as her friend went on about this new experience. Smoking cigarettes and pacing impatiently, Cornelia chattered nonstop about how wonderful it had been as she watched other planes, large and small, land and take off.

Finally, Cornelia was able to begin her first lesson. Her teacher was Aubrey, a handsome soft-spoken twenty-eight-year-old with a Clark Gable mustache and eight years of flying experience. They went up in a Luscombe 50, a 20-foot plane with a 35-foot wingspan and a 50-horsepower engine. It weighed 650 pounds empty and cruised at 96 miles an hour. As they took off and rose, Aubrey, sitting in the right-hand seat, explained the basics—the stick, the pedals, the rudder, the gauges, the concept of lift. Then, at an altitude of 2,000 feet, he turned the controls over to Cornelia, telling her to use the stick to keep the plane steady. She later wrote, "I had a terrible time and finally turned to him in desperation. He was most amused. 'Soon,' he chuckled, 'you won't even think about the plane's being level. You will feel it as automatically as you drive a car.' That seemed impossible then."

Cornelia did not rush to tell her family about her new passion, and with good reason. When Dudley learned she was taking lessons he was outraged. "How dare you fly," he asked her, "knowing your father forbade us to do it?"

"Daddy gave that oath to you boys," she told him, "not to me."

Eight

D r. Fort died early on Good Friday morning, March 22, 1940, three days after his sixty-eighth birthday. There were few in the city who did not know of his accomplishments. Tributes poured in from business associates and from the newspapers, and the city's elite gathered at Fortland on Saturday afternoon for his funeral. Nashville's most exclusive cemetery, Mt. Olivet, was the site of a snowy burial. Much of the city mourned his passing. "It is with real regret," said the *Tennessean,* "that the end of such a full and constructive life is noted."

Cornelia, while saddened by her father's death, worried more about her mother. Mrs. Fort had no sense of her husband's business dealings, and her life of constant motion had always found its anchor in him and the estate his success provided. Cornelia encouraged her to rely on her sons for help in running Fortland.

Cornelia herself was not slowed by her father's death. Flying was in part a celebration of the sense of freedom she had long cultivated, and she filled her days with it. She took naturally to the air. From the beginning, Aubrey said, she was "competent and completely unafraid." She was also eager, hoping to learn as fast as possible. Aubrey, holding that lessons should be spaced out so students could better retain what they'd learned, dictated a more studied pace. Over the next few weeks, it took Cornelia nine flying days to gain the eight hours of air time necessary to solo; Aubrey said she would have been ready at five or six hours.

Even between lessons, Cornelia wanted to be in the air. She spent a great deal of time at Berry Field, where an airplane called the Stinson 105 was being produced. One afternoon she and Aubrey were standing in front of a hangar when a Stinson representative taxied up in one. He got out and approached them.

"You wanna fly that Stinson?" he said to Aubrey. "That's the finest airplane you've ever flown."

"I don't care anything about it, especially," Aubrey said.

"It's got these eyebrows on the wings," the Stinson man said, "and it's virtually spin-proof."

"Aaaah," said Aubrey. He turned to Cornelia and said in a low voice, "Ain't no such thing as a spin-proof airplane."

The Stinson rep heard him and said, "Be my guest."

"OK," said Aubrey. He turned to Cornelia. "You wanna go do a spin?"

Without a word Cornelia sprinted toward the hangar. Aubrey, who was never in much of a hurry, ambled along behind her. As he neared the doorway, Cornelia came running out with a parachute on each shoulder. "Here's yours," she said. They put on their chutes and climbed in, Aubrey at the controls.

They headed north, gained altitude, and circled back toward the field. Aubrey did a stall, kicked full right rudder, and gave the throttle a light touch. The plane rolled over and, sure enough, went into a spin. Aubrey pulled the plane out and went back and landed.

"Oh, you had to use power to do it," the Stinson rep said, referring to Aubrey's touch of the throttle.

"Listen," Aubrey said, as Cornelia stood alongside, "ninety percent of the spins that kill people and tear up airplanes are done just after takeoff, when you're using power to climb." The rep huffed again, got back in the plane, and taxied away. Cornelia took in the entire episode, trying to learn everything she could from the flight and the conversation.

On April 27, she and Aubrey met at the airport for her solo in the Luscombe 50. As Aubrey watched, she made three take-offs and landings, overjoyed that she was finally in the air on her own.

Cornelia rushed home, thrilled at her accomplishment. She leaped from her car and ran to her mother, who was in her garden, wearing gloves and a large straw hat, cutting daffodils for the house and laying them in a basket. Mrs. Fort listened impassively as Cornelia described the flight. When she had finished, Mrs. Fort continued snipping and spoke without looking up.

"How very nice, dear," she said. "Now you won't have to do that again."

But Cornelia had found something that demanded and deserved her full passion, concentration, and commitment. There could be no half measures. Cornelia the lackluster student disappeared. She was consumed, eager to learn everything she could, to throw herself completely into flying. Already it felt like more than a hobby, more even than a job. She had a calling. She hung a wooden propeller over the doorway in her bedroom. It dominated the tiny room the way flying had already come to dominate her life.

Cornelia would arrive at the airport on many mornings wearing a short-sleeved summer dress and carrying her big purse. There was nothing flashy about her. "She could have had a Cadillac," Aubrey said, "but she was driving a Chevrolet. If she wanted something, she'd buy it and pay cash for it, but she wasn't putting on any show or 'Look what I've got' or 'what I did' or 'what I accomplished' or anything else. That didn't enter her mind." Her one extravagance was the flying itself. Cornelia flew fifteen or more hours a week at five or six dollars an hour. "She was writing checks right and left for flying time," said Aubrey, "and it was running up a pretty good sum, too."

Cornelia set out to become a good pilot, but she had no female role models in Tennessee in 1940. In aviation, as in many fields, women had never had an easy time of it. When the army had come to the city to tout flying at the old Hampton Field in 1919, there was one woman among the many reporters taken for rides. *The Nashville Banner's* Mary Stahlman waited until mid-afternoon, when nearly all the men had gone, before asking for her turn.

"Lady," said one of the pilots, "we have orders not to take women." She nevertheless persuaded him, signing her name as *M. C. Stahlman* to cover her tracks. She later rode with one of Jersey Ringel's pilots, doing loops and an engine-off dive with him at a show.

Flying whenever she could out of Berry Field, Cornelia quickly approached fifty hours of flight time. She needed a dual cross-country flight for her license, so, on June 17, Aubrey accompanied her to St. Louis and back, watching as she constantly checked her map.

"She'd say, 'We're going right over Clarksville, right on course,'" he recalled. "A little later she'd find something else on her map, and she'd say, 'Yeah, that's right where it's supposed to be,' and we'd get up to the Mississippi River and she'd look at her map again and look around: 'Yeah, there's that bend in the river on my map. I'm right on course.'"

Back at home, she took Governor Cooper for rides in the Luscombe on consecutive evenings. He had been among the many family friends at her debutante ball, and the two went out together both nights. The governor was a full five inches shorter than Cornelia, and the dates had little to recommend them. The governor noted in his diary that he enjoyed Friday's date "only so-so," while on Saturday night Cornelia "was too sleepy to be good company." Nevertheless, in honor of the flights he had taken with her—they were his first without a parachute, he said—he named Cornelia a captain in the Tennessee National Guard.

On Sunday, Cornelia told Aubrey she wanted another long flight, and though he reminded her that she didn't need another to qualify for her license, she convinced him to accompany her to Louisville. "I just want to be good," she told him. "I want to be thorough. Being adequate isn't good enough."

When Cornelia reached fifty hours, Aubrey signed her off to be tested for a private license. "She came back all smiles," he said, "with the license in her hand."

It was time to celebrate, and Cornelia called about a dozen friends together. Most were her new flying friends, with only Jack Caldwell and Betty representing the group she'd grown up with. They met at Fortland, and Cornelia, who had never had the opportunity to indulge her acquired taste for the occasional cocktail at home, served drinks to her guests. Prohibition had been repealed in Tennessee in 1939, but only Dr. Fort's death lifted prohibition at Fortland. After decades, the big house was dry no longer. The precedent established, Cornelia would bring friends over often during the summer. By October, the *Tennessean* was referring to Cornelia as "the hostess of innumerable swell house parties at Fortland."

Cornelia had earned her license more quickly than any Nashville student before her, and she set out to use it. She later wrote:

> Nothing ever meant so much to me as my private license; it was the first big step up. I took the privileges of that little white piece of paper very seriously: "The holder may fly anywhere within the limits of Continental United States." In the first week I flew well over 2,000 miles. I must admit that lunching in St. Louis, breakfasting in Louisville, flying down to a cocktail party in the Mississippi Delta was very exciting.

In August, Cornelia took her usual summer trip to New England to visit relatives. As she settled in at her uncle J. Dudley Clark's house in Boston, though, it was against a backdrop of rising international tensions. Hitler's war machine was still in high gear; France was surrendering to the Germans. Cornelia, who hoped additional flying skills would only make her more valuable should the nation enter the war, made a quick trip to Maine, where she earned a seaplane license. She spent much of her time in Boston at East Boston Airport and became the subject of a lengthy August 27 piece by *Boston Daily Record* columnist George W. Clarke, who said she was "saving up to buy her own plane."

Back home, she had dreams of starting a flying service with Aubrey. "I'll buy all the airplanes and equipment and everything," she told him. "I'll pay cash for it if you'll run it and be chief pilot and boss. And then as soon as I get my ratings [her commercial and instructor's licenses], I'll help you, and if we make a profit we'll just split it."

Nothing ever came of the idea. U.S. participation in the war seemed inevitable, and Aubrey told Cornelia he would be joining the military before long.

Cornelia wanted to fly every plane she could. She jumped at the chance to drive Aubrey the thirty miles to Murfreesboro, where he was going to take up a Curtiss Robin, a 25-foot plane with a wingspan of 41 feet and a cruising speed of 102 mph. Once he got it airborne and level, he slipped out of the front seat and eased back along the windows, his hand holding the stick in position while she slid into his place. She took the stick, fastened her belt, and flew the plane for twenty minutes or so before Aubrey took it back in for a landing.

Cornelia also looked for little ways to increase the time she could spend in the air. Fortland was about seven miles by surface streets from Berry Field, but less than three by plane, so she asked if Aubrey would fly over to the farm, pick her up in the morning, and take her back at night, using a spot at the far end of the pasture for a landing strip.

There was just one problem with the arrangement. Once they left for Berry Field, Cornelia's car sat in the pasture all day. As they flew over the farm on occasion, they could see the Forts' prize-winning Jersey cows gathered around the Chevy. It turned out they were licking it, attracted to the taste of the paint. By the end of summer, Cornelia had to have the car repainted.

Cornelia and Aubrey saw much of each other that summer and fall, as she relentlessly gained flight time, trying to improve her skills. "I had a lot of admiration for her ability and her cool-ness, her levelheadedness," he said. "She was by far and gone the best female student I ever had, and she was better than a whole lot of the men students. She was just plain good, and she didn't have to work at it too hard, either. She could just grasp it."

There was never a hint of romance—Aubrey was married at the time—although he said he suspected she may have had a mild crush on him. Their relationship, from day one, was about flying. During the long periods they spent together they discussed every aspect of it: other pilots, equipment, airports, Cornelia's dreams, Aubrey's background. Aubrey had been in the audience at the fairgrounds in 1921 when Jersey Ringel and his Flying Circus had thrilled and terrified the crowd. He had watched, mesmerized, not by Jersey or the pilot but by the machine itself, awed by its movement through the air. Three years earlier, at age six, he had heard for the first time "the wonderful sounds of whirling pro-pellers" as two planes flew over his home in Spring Hill, Tennes-see. "Those few minutes were definitely the high point of my young life," he said. "I determined that I would grow up to be a flying machine driver."

He in turn passed that magic calling on to Cornelia, and now her flights were becoming just such an inspiration to others. She became a frequent source of wonder, flying over the farms and neighborhoods in the area. An aircraft buzzing over a farm field in 1940 was a rare sight, and people stopped what they were doing to watch. "I'll bet that's Cornelia Fort" was a common saying when a plane was overhead in Nashville. In October, she was asked to address the American Association of University Women on "Youth and Aviation."

Cornelia wanted to learn aerial acrobatics—stunt flying—and Aubrey was happy to teach her. They went up in a Waco UPF-7, a 220-horsepower open-cockpit two-seater with a 30-foot wingspan and a cruising speed of 115 mph. It had a full panel of instruments in each of two cockpits, which sat one behind the other. As he tightened her belt, pulling it more snugly than usual, Aubrey warned, "This may hurt a little, but you'll have to put up with it. I don't want you falling out."

Aubrey always began a student's first acrobatics lesson by getting to a good altitude, rolling the plane over, and holding it there. It was an experience that startled pretty much everybody. Since this was an open-cockpit plane, his riders would suddenly find themselves upside down over a couple of thousand feet of air, falling a long inch or so until they were caught and held in place by the four-inch waist belt. Aubrey would look in the mirror and see their hands flailing for support that wasn't there, a momentary look of panic on their faces.

Not Cornelia. When Aubrey rolled the plane over, he looked in the mirror, only to see her giving him a little wave, hanging by the belt. "She didn't have any nerves, I don't reckon," he said. "She never showed any."

As she learned the stalls, loops, rolls, and spins that make up aerobatics, Cornelia experienced a new level of delight. Cutting through the air, pushing off in a tight little turn, or soaring over the top into the lazy start of a stall, it was as though the plane had become an extension of her own body. On the ground she might be tall and awkward, conscious of the limitations her large frame imposed, but once she lifted off she became quite simply the daughter of the air, a creature as graceful and at home as any hawk or eagle.

She was also a daredevil. Cornelia wanted to take Fortland foreman Charles Kinle for a ride, but he wasn't sure he wanted to be airborne with a girl who rode horses with such abandon. She would fly over the farm, smiling and waving as she leaned out of the open cockpit of the Waco, which looked to Charles "like there wasn't a whole lot to it." Then she'd land nearby and ask if he was ready to take his ride yet. "She tried her best to get me in that airplane," he said.

One summer afternoon, Charles and some of his workers were taking up hay when they heard the telltale buzz of Cornelia's plane in the distance. Often she came from the east, the direction of the airport. This time it was from the west, from beyond the railroad bridge that crossed the river near Fortland's border with Shelby Park. "I heard that thing," he said, "and I looked, and it was coming *under* the bridge, in between those piers, about halfway between the trestle and the river. She came up and made two or three flipovers—just rolled it around."

Charles was certain now that he would not be taking Cornelia up on her offer. "I wouldn't have been in that thing for no kind of money," he said.

And so, after all her father had planned for her—after Ward-Belmont, with its riding stables and tough academics, its sororities and dances; after Ogontz, with its structure and military discipline; after her debut and Nashville's literary and social clubs, all designed to help guide a young woman toward a proper life—Cornelia had found her place in the air with the Jersey Ringels of the world. What's more, she had regained the straightforward joy she had known as a child, the joy adolescence and her discomfort with Nashville's rigid social patterns had stolen from her.

There came a time that fall, though, when Aubrey thought Cornelia's enthusiasm had overcome her judgment. On the Tuesday before Thanksgiving, they were flying into tiny Mt. Pleasant, Tennessee, when Aubrey took the controls and did a spin "for the boys that hung around the airport." As Aubrey talked to his friends after landing, Cornelia slipped back into the plane. She took it up, gained some altitude, did the spin she had just watched Aubrey do, and then brought it in for a landing. It was the only time Aubrey thought she had ever pushed the envelope too far, and he took her to task for it. She simply stood her ground, as she had when Dudley challenged her about flying despite her father's objections.

"But, Aubrey," she said, "I'm a major too."

"She meant," Aubrey explained, "that she had the same kind of license I had."

Cornelia and Aubrey took a final short trip together on January 4. On February 4, Aubrey would report to the South East Air Corps Training Center, an army contract school in Albany, Georgia. As he said goodbye to Cornelia, he realized they had never had an extended conversation about anything except flying. "That's all she ever talked about with me," he said, "either asking questions and wanting answers or talking about what she had done."

Except for one dinner and two lunches at Fortland, they had never had anything that might be construed as social contact either. And yet they had developed a deep and genuine bond. "There's something about teaching a person to fly," Aubrey said. "You become part of each other."

Nine

ornelia received her commercial license on February 8, 1941, becoming only the second Nashville woman ever to do so. By March 10, she had earned her instructor's rating and took a job teaching for local flyer Garland Pack. Cornelia's family background and her growing local celebrity as a flyer led the Sunday *Tennessean* to announce, under a three-column headline and photo, the launching of Cornelia's career on March 16.

"Women are needed in aviation and can be an important factor in the national defense program," she told the paper. "Women can do in this country what they have been doing in England— ferrying planes from factories to airports, flying the mail, and doing transport work for the government. Every woman who flies releases a man to fight."

War with Germany had indeed opened the skies to women in England. The Battle of Britain, just months earlier, had taken an enormous toll on British planes and flyers, and women were ferrying planes for the British Air Transport Auxiliary. In the United States, civilian men were delivering planes, and Cornelia, like many other women pilots, was hoping for the chance to join that effort.

In the meantime, she looked for other opportunities, something that would offer a bigger challenge and the opportunity to travel. While she feared that being a woman would hurt her chances, Cornelia wrote to every flying school in the country, hoping for a teaching job. In short order, she received a telegram from the Massey-Ransom Flying Service of Fort Collins, Colorado. It read:

MR. CORNELIA FORT. YOU ARE ACCEPTED AS A FLIGHT
INSTRUCTOR. REPORT AT ONCE.

In tears, Cornelia took the telegram to her mother. "Look, Mother," she said. "They think Cornelia is a man's name. I knew no one would hire a female flight instructor."

Mrs. Fort was still not crazy about the fact that her daughter was flying, but she knew how much it meant to Cornelia. "Wire them back," she said, "and tell them you are a woman pilot." She studied her daughter, who was weeping the hysterical tears of someone who feels a dream evaporating. "And have Epperson take you down to the Western Union office. You are in no condition to drive."

With Epperson driving, Cornelia went off to the telegraph office and sent the wire. The next day the reply came:

MR. OR MISS OR MRS. FORT. WE DO NOT CARE WHAT YOU
ARE IF YOU CAN TEACH FLYING. REPORT AT ONCE.

This time Cornelia cried tears of joy.

Cornelia spread the news and prepared for the trip to Fort Collins. Exhilarated by flying and by this new opportunity, she informed her mother she would be driving to her new job, with her Irish setter, Kevin, as company. Mrs. Fort was horrified. It was totally improper for a young girl—Cornelia was, after all, barely twenty-two—to drive unchaperoned across the country, and it was simply not going to happen. Mrs. Fort insisted that Epperson accompany her. He did so, listening to Cornelia deliver a long cross-country monologue about flying and then depositing her and her car safely at the Armstrong Hotel and boarding a bus for the trip home.

For Cornelia, as for the nation as a whole, there was no escaping the war in Europe. She had watched events there closely throughout her first year of flying. France's surrender had been the culmination of a long string of events. A month after signing a nonaggression pact with the Soviet Union in August 1939, Germany invaded Poland. Britain and France in turn declared war on Germany. Russia seized eastern Poland, attacked Finland, and overran the Baltic states. In the spring of 1940, Germany overran Denmark and the Low Countries before taking France. Now, as Cornelia moved into the Martin Apartments in Fort Collins, Germany and Italy were taking over the Balkans.

Cornelia's new job owed its existence to Hitler. The Roosevelt administration, recognizing the growing threat of Germany's air force, had established the Civilian Pilot Training Program in 1938. Spearheaded by Army Air Force commander General Henry Harley "Hap" Arnold, the program was designed to enlarge the U.S. aviation industry and teach young Americans to fly in preparation for the nation's probable entry into the war. Although the military had thus far resisted using female pilots, women were welcome in the CPTP. The AAF had fewer than 1,000 officers and was adding only 300 a year, while Arnold figured the country would soon need 100,000 trained pilots. Ground school was often conducted in college classrooms, with nearby airstrips used for the flying. The Massey-Ransom Flying Service, one of many private firms contracted for CPTP instruction, was scrambling for pilots and welcomed Cornelia's application.

Otis T. Massey and Harry Ransom were young flyers from Denver who had come in 1936 to Fort Collins, a small college town set amid the region's farms and ranches. They opened a flying school just west of town at Christman Field, at the edge of the foothills of the Rockies. The field was owned by the college—Colorado State College of Agriculture and the Mechanic Arts—which would later become Colorado State University. Its gravel landing strip was 5,000 feet above sea level, and the mountains immediately to its west swept upward another 2,000 feet. Farther west, they climbed to 12,000 or 13,000 feet, and the winds rushing down from them often made day-to-day flying tricky.

Massey and Ransom had a small fleet of Cub, Lovecraft, and Luscombe airplanes, housed in three new 60-by-80-foot hangars built specifically for the CPTP. Cornelia, one of several new instructors and the only woman, taught new students primarily in the Luscombe, a plane she had flown in Nashville.

Cornelia threw herself into her work. Most of her attention was on flying, and she told the others relatively little about herself. Her students, at least, had no idea about her background. "I didn't think she had a nickel in her jeans," said Vance Pinkerton, who took lessons from Cornelia. "I remember her as being in striped bib overalls, the kind blacksmiths used to wear, with her dark glasses on top of her head. She was a darn nice girl, and I thought she was just an ordinary kid coming along trying to make a nickel."

Still, her passion for the air allowed at least one student to glimpse another side of her. A year and a half later she would receive a letter—it was unsigned—that read, in part:

> My first "ride" when we flew to Greeley for the "chutes." Your laughter the first time we "spun." The moonlight of the highway when we drove home from the rodeo. Your tears and kiss when I soloed.
>
> Please don't mistake this for a romantic love note. It is the note of a youth inspired and awed by a marvelous woman. I enjoyed those days and you more than you could ever know.

In mid-July, Cornelia flew to Mobile to join her Sarah Lawrence friends for the wedding of Ann Perdue. When she returned to Fort Collins, she poured herself into writing an article for the *Alumnae News* about her new life. For the first time, she described in detail what it was like to fly and what she had seen and done and felt. While she hadn't written anything formal in some time, she had been keeping her diary religiously, and now she was writing with real passion. The article appeared late in 1941.

LADY-BIRD
by Cornelia Fort, '39

If only I had some answer, any answer, to the eternal question "How did you start flying?" but I don't. Frankly, I don't even remember, but I began, in weeks and months, a very short time ago.

Looking back to little more than a year ago, it seems very much like the famous two roads that "diverged in a yellow wood." I shudder when I think how easily I might have missed that road that led to the airplanes, to the misty summer sunrises and the aching profitless hours of practice with the sun beating down—and to all the little remembered bits of happiness that fit into the flying pattern.

But let me refute at the start the too-common notion that flying is glamorous. Too many girls have entered aviation with only a desire for shining white coveralls, a helmet and goggles, and the "fine free wind" in their hair. And it is these sorry sisters who have caused the rest of us to fight, and fight hard, for every ounce of recognition and respect that we have earned. Flying isn't glamorous or even adventurous in the ordinary sense of the word. It is for the most part heartbreaking, backbreaking work. The adventures we all have which make such wonderful stories afterwards seem at the time only desperate moments when we were completely helpless, moments for which we would gladly turn in our flying suits to have done without.

You will ask me why we fly, and that's a question very few pilots can answer coherently. "For room and board" is the only logical answer; further explanations are always vague, because we can't manage to put into words what it is that really keeps us at it. There's not one of us, no matter how tired we may be of everything connected with airplanes, whose head won't perk up at the sound of an engine overhead, whose eyes won't light up as a shining plane roars down the runway. And that's the only answer there is; in brief, the trite phrase: "It gets under your skin, deep down inside."

Everyone is more or less interested in flying—more interested than in ditch-digging, less interested than most pilots, who will talk flying round the clock to anyone who shows a flicker of enthusiasm to the subject. For a girl to fly is, of course, still unusual enough to provoke plenty of conversation. The fact that I am a pilot precedes me wherever I go, and reactions are fascinating, especially since I started instructing.

The question I am asked most often is whether my students (all boys) resent a female instructor. Strangely enough they don't seem to. I think the explanation is in the psychological setup. They are so completely helpless at first, and after leading them by the hand for eight hours up to the climax of soloing I have made them so dependent upon me that they seldom think of me as anything other than the instructor.

She then recalled her first lesson and her moment of "desperation," after Aubrey turned the stick over to her and then reassured her that eventually she would get the feel of it.

That seemed impossible then; but now I find myself laughing at my fledglings as they try frantically to keep the plane level. That was my first introduction to the word "feel," that all-important intangible attribute that distinguishes a good pilot from a mediocre one. And it doesn't take long to discover whether a boy has the makings of a good flyer, just about two days. One student, who backhanded the stick and who struggled over everything that should have come quite easily to him, turned to me in distress. "You know, Miss Fort," he said, "I just can't seem to get used to this flying business. I'm so used to handling a tractor." And to the end of time that's the way he will fly—as if that lovely instrument of precision were a Caterpillar tractor!

She recalled the joy of earning her license and the exhilaration of her busy first week of flying.

And then came my first experience of the ugly side of flying, running into "weather" without instruments.

We earthbound creatures are so used to having a constant reference point, the ground, that we can't realize what it means to be without it, as one is in fog, which wraps the plane in a thick blanket, completely destroying one's sense of equilibrium. This situation is so serious that there is a law to cover it: "If the pilot is at any time unable to see the ground for more than 3 minutes at a time he must go on instruments, return to his base, or immediately set down." There are times, however, when one can do none of these. One has no instruments, the weather has closed in, and there are mountains underneath. Incredible as it sounds, one doesn't know whether the plane is upside down, dragging a wing (which leads to a spin), or spinning. Even if you do realize that something is wrong, it is terribly difficult to remedy the situation. A spin is perfectly safe and easy with sufficient altitude to recover, but pilots spinning out of fog seldom do recover.

The first time this happened to me I was in mountain country flying a passenger down to wave at his girl. Fortunately, I was flying a stable plane, and luckily I decided to let the plane almost fly itself. When I finally decided to go back, even though the weather looked as bad behind me, I saw the compass swing around 180 degrees but had no sensation of turning. That stood my hair on end; I have never been so relieved as I was when I saw the home port after I finally broke through.

I've had more than my share of "weather," and more than my share of luck. Last year I ferried a ship from the factory in Pennsylvania to Nashville, across the Allegheny Mountains, which are among the roughest in the country. I was flying straight across the mountains when the fog came rolling in. I flew for an hour, seeing the mountain ridges beneath me but none of the valleys. The fog kept getting worse and worse, and finally it closed in altogether. Without a radio, without landmarks, and with only an hour's fuel left, I was far from happy. Suddenly I saw a little hole in the clouds and a patch of valley 400 feet down. I cocked the plane up and slipped it straight down, and came out of the fog at about 600 feet. Looking around I found a lonely wheat field and landed as hastily as possible.

Little did the Elmer Smiths know they were going to be my hosts for two nights and days when they came running through the snow to see if I was safe. Nothing about me impressed them half as much as that I knew vaguely where I was. (Nothing impressed the sixteen-year-old daughter as much as that I had actually seen and heard Benny Goodman!) They were very kind and friendly. It was 10 above zero in that Quaker community, and I was indeed grateful for their hospitality.

Having been raised on a farm, I felt I should try to talk about crops. The farmer beamed at me and remarked that I must have lived in the country. I modestly replied that I had and that my father had been interested in thoroughbred Jersey cattle. When I said that we had had about two hundred of these the farmer looked at me in amazement. "How in the world can you leave home with so much milking to be done?" he asked. That question put to me in all sincerity rather floored me, but I managed to say feebly that I had three brothers!

After being grounded in Harrisburg, and again in Virginia, I flew wearily into Nashville ten days later, convinced that trains and buses were the only sane means of transportation. Yet the very next day I flew to Memphis for three weeks of advanced training. When I got my commercial license I thought that I would be satisfied, but this flying is like an awful thirst; one wants to learn more and more and to accumulate ratings. The more experience I get the less I seem to know, which is terribly discouraging.

I came out here to Fort Collins, Colorado, to get altitude experience—the hardest flying there is. We are a mile high, which is higher than most light plane pilots ever get at sea level. I'm flying off the side of the Rocky Mountains where the air is tricky and vicious; one learns plenty and fast. A year ago if anyone had told me that I'd ever care about the workings of a carburetor I would have laughed in his face, and if that same person had told me that I would get up at 4:30 A.M. and work straight through until almost 8 P.M. daily for six months, I'd have thought him crazy. Yet one student who really aches to learn, one sun-drenched flight at sunrise, one trip chasing a rainbow, one little girl who claps her hands and shouts "Roller coaster," one cool, deeply quiet flight up the canyon at dusk are perhaps reasons enough.

All of us have the wanderlust. We either fly because we have it or acquire it because we fly. And that's the magic of it for me—to step into a plane at noon and get out among palm trees four hours later; to swim in the Gulf and the next day to be 1,000 miles away. I believe, too, that it's a character-builder; there is absolutely no one to rely on, no help, no advice, no comfort. One's decisions and the skill that flows out of one's hands are the only realities. And that aloneness, which is so really terrifying at first, becomes eventually something useful and free and warmly good.

Ten

By July, fighting in the Pacific had intensified and Cornelia was looking for a way to contribute to what was, if not a war effort, at least preparation for one. She earned a ground instructor's certificate, which allowed her to begin classroom teaching, on August 5. A few weeks later she received a letter from the Andrew Flying Service, which operated out of the John Rodgers Airport in Honolulu, offering her an instructor's job. Knowing there were what she termed "millions—thousands anyway—of embryo pilots" among the city's military personnel and defense workers, she jumped at the chance. Cornelia desperately wanted her flying to mean something. With this new job, she would be training sailors and factory workers to fly, helping perhaps to beef up the country's air forces at a critical time. After visits to Nashville, San Francisco, and Los Angeles, she boarded the steamship *Mariposa* on September 20 for the trip to Honolulu.

The *Mariposa* steamed into the islands of postcards and tourists' dreams. As it rounded Diamond Head, the ship was met by a tugboat whose occupants climbed aboard, bearing flower leis. Cornelia and the other passengers lined the deck railings to watch the standard dockside spectacle unfold. As the Aloha Tower, the clock tower that rose imposingly above the docks and warehouses, came closer, the Royal Hawaiian Band played "Aloha 'Oe" against a backdrop of waving streamers and people carrying still more leis.

This was one of the two Honolulus that coexisted uneasily at the time. It was filled with the sight and smell of flowers, with fresh fruit and fish in little markets, with balmy breezes and fair-weather clouds, lovely sunsets, lush green forests, and huge expanses of pineapple and sugarcane. There were Oriental servants, fine restaurants, good hotels, and clubs with live popular and Hawaiian music.

The other Honolulu was nothing less than a full-scale military boom town. Japanese expansionism in Southeast Asia had prompted President Roosevelt to shift the U.S. fleet from Southern California to Pearl Harbor in May 1940. By the time Cornelia arrived, the city was crawling with sailors, many of whom were out on shipboard maneuvers during the week and on the beaches and in the city's bars and restaurants on the weekends.

The navy was not alone. The Army Air Force occupied Wheeler Field, northwest of Pearl Harbor; Hickam Field, a major bomber base a little to its southeast; and Bellows Field, a small training base on the eastern shore of Oahu. Other facilities around the island included a marine base at Ewa, Kaneohe Naval Air Station, Fort Shafter with its Tripler Army Hospital, and a handful of radar sites. Military personnel had long considered Hawaii choice duty, as it featured everything from world-famous sand and surf to a teeming red-light district, but they also knew that a flare-up with the Japanese was always a possibility.

Cornelia witnessed sporadic antiaircraft fire and learned that gray puffs of smoke indicated practice shells—smoke from the real ones was black. Once a week or so, the power would go out with no warning, pitching everything into darkness. After a few moments, the radio stations would announce that another blackout drill had been completed.

Cornelia found an apartment in Waikiki, a beachfront community southeast of the city that was a playground for American tourists, including a generous sprinkling of movie stars, and settled in. On Friday, October 3, she wrote Dudley:

Dear Brother Dudley,

Thank you for your last two letters. I've been moving around so much I have hardly had time to write Mother.

In your letter to me in Colo. you mentioned that you hoped I was going to church while away from home. For six months there I worked all but two Sundays & on those two I slept. Don't worry about my soul—I realize how wonderful our childhood was, how lucky beyond hope of written word we are to have had such parents.

Honolulu is pretty wonderful—except for the defense workers & enlisted men & the only thing wrong with them is that there are so many of them. Warm but not hot & cool breezes from the sea at nite. It rains on & off all day but lightly—no one pays any attention to it at all—we don't even stop flying.

My apt. is right across from the Royal Hawaiian Hotel & consequently from Waikiki. The surf is marvelous but the beach is bitterly disappointing—narrow & dirty.

The flowers are marvelous—great banks of them outside my door. The little Chinese maid fills the apt. with them every day.

This is an excellent place to work—a good organization & good planes. I'm flying more open ships (stunting biplanes) than I've ever flown before. It's all a lot of fun.

The people are friendly & Democratic in a very good sense. I wish you all could come over—I'll show you everything from Waikiki to a hula.

Living costs are out of sight though—eggs 84¢ a dozen & butter 67¢ per lb. The same can of pineapple juice that cost 27¢ in Colo. costs 33¢ here. Figure it out.

Love,
Cornelia

The military personnel and defense workers did indeed constitute a spawning ground for "embryo pilots." Oahu's flying services saw a steady stream of military men who viewed flying lessons as a route to advancement and who had the money to pay for them. Cornelia, the second woman instructor on the island, was busy from the start.

The Andrew Flying Service was owned by Ole Andrew, a lanky, perpetually smiling Swede in his late thirties who generally employed six or eight instructors, including moonlighting navy pilots. In late 1941 his roster included a Japanese instructor named Roy Umaki and a tall, thin Arizona native who was part American Indian and whom everyone called Cowboy. The service operated out of John Rodgers Airport, Honolulu's civilian field, about a mile from Hickam Field and adjacent to Pearl Harbor. It had been finished just a year earlier, and Ole's employees stayed busy giving lessons and hopping passengers around the island.

Oahu presented yet another set of flying conditions for Cornelia. A key element was the way the winds shifted during the day. At dawn, the cooled land created an onshore breeze that would often counteract the trade winds, leaving the air calm and quiet. As the land warmed, the trade winds would resume, flowing briskly from the northeast until, by midafternoon, they would often be a real problem for Ole's Piper Cubs and Interstate Cadets. Many of these and other tiny planes couldn't be flown in the afternoon because the wind was simply too strong for them.

Cornelia and the other pilots used a gravel runway that ran about 3,000 feet from southwest to northeast. A marsh of sugarcane and algaroba, occupied by mongooses, mynah birds, and other wildlife, lay on its southeast side, while hangars lined the northwest. The Hawaiian Airlines hangar sat about 1,000 feet from the southwest end of the runway. Beside an empty lot to the northeast sat a restaurant, followed by the general aviation hangars, with Andrew's, the largest, first in line. The airport had no control tower, and the smaller planes had no radios, so Hawaiian Airlines sounded a huge siren to alert small planes when one of its large airliners was coming in.

One of Cornelia's first acquaintances in Hawaii was Betty Guild, a beautiful twenty-year-old Honolulu resident. Betty, who had learned to fly at fifteen, sent out billing statements and handled other paperwork for Ole in exchange for flying time. She found Cornelia to be "happy-go-lucky, full of fun and optimism." The two of them often drank Cokes or coffee in the airport restaurant. Sometimes, over Chinese food and drinks in a restaurant or night spot, they shared their childhood and coming-of-age stories, finding common ground in the fact that both of them had looked outside the Junior League crowd for fulfillment.

"I think one of the reasons Cornelia and I became good friends," Betty said, "was because I was really almost ostracized when I took up flying. That was something nice girls didn't do.

My cousin was head of the Junior League [in Honolulu] and they wanted me to join, but they told me I'd have to give up flying to do it because it would interfere with my volunteer work."

They talked too about Amelia Earhart, whom Betty had met when she was fourteen and already "wound up on flying." Betty attended a lecture by Earhart, who asked if she would like to come out the next day to watch her take off on a flight toward California, a route that had never been successfully flown. "My father took me out to Wheeler Field," Betty recalled, "and she was such a soft-voiced, gentle, ethereal kind of person. But she started to take off and there was something wrong with the plane, and she taxied back and they pulled it into the hangar, and you have never heard such language in your life as she used. My father, who never swore, just ushered me right out of the hangar, and that was the only time I saw her."

A year later, at fifteen, Betty began sneaking flying lessons. She would tell her parents she was going to the beach and hitch-hike to the airport instead. After two years, she finally told her father, who agreed to sign the papers that allowed her to pursue her license. Now, with her limited commercial license, Betty regularly took customers on morning runs that Cornelia soon joined.

Flying open-cockpit biplanes, four or five pilots would take tourists on a lazy ninety-minute loop to the west side of the island just after sunrise. It was a beautiful flight, over pineapple fields and banana trees and dew-covered vegetation sparkling under clear skies. Their destination was an old hotel called the Haleiwa, nestled amid ponds and greenery at the edge of the ocean.

The planes would buzz the hotel, which would send a little boy in a station wagon—a "banana wagon"—to meet them at the grass landing strip nearby. The entire group would eat a big breakfast and then take off again for the half-hour flight back over Pearl Harbor to Hickam Field.

Such was the nonchalance of youth that most of their flying was done without parachutes or flotation devices. "The only time we had chutes on was when we did acrobatics," Betty recalled.

The beauty of those days would stay with Cornelia for the rest of her life. She would speak later of the times when she flew "up into the extinct volcano Haleakala on the island of Maui and saw the gray-green pineapple fields slope down to the cloud-dappled blueness of the Pacific."

Cornelia enjoyed the work as well, and before long she had all she could handle. There were frequent sightseeing flights and four or five 45-minute lessons a day, for which the students paid $15 apiece. At the beginning, most of her students were male—defense workers, soldiers, and sailors who saved their money for flying and dreamed of joining the Air Corps—but it wasn't long before some young women started showing up as well. Betty remembered them as being well-mannered, attractive, and in their early to middle twenties. They were well dressed and well groomed without being flashy or gaudy, and it was obvious they had money; some came for lessons in a black limousine with a Filipino chauffeur. Betty and Cornelia had no idea who they were or why they wanted to learn to fly. There were, otherwise, very few women flying in the islands.

Gradually, though, the women missed lessons here and there, simply not showing up for time they had booked. Ole, who was, after all, running a business, began calling the phone numbers they'd left to find out where they were, and he always ended up talking with a "house mother." Finally, the story emerged: the students were prostitutes, who had come over from the mainland to service Honolulu's military population. They had been set up in houses around the city, and navy doctors were even inspecting the new establishments to make sure they didn't pose too much of a health risk. Apparently, the women figured flying lessons would be a fun way to spend their ready cash.

Cornelia's life revolved around flying, as it had in Colorado; she had little social life. She and Betty might eat dinner occasionally at Lau Yee Chai's, Waikiki's hottest night spot, chatting and listening to the band play hits like "Deep Purple" or "Frenesi." There were occasional touches of glamour, as when Betty's friend, heiress Doris Duke, and her date Monty Whitehead, who had been a quarterback at the Naval Academy and was now serving as ensign on the USS *Arizona,* joined them for dinner.

But Cornelia avoided nearby Waikiki Beach, which was usually packed with tourists and any soldiers and sailors who happened to have the day off. The military men could be a wild bunch, anxious to have what fun they could on paychecks that began at about $20 a month. A ten-cent bus ride or a quarter cab ride downtown would land them on Hotel Street, where the Army and Navy YMCA was located, as were tattoo parlors and the popular Black Cat Cafe, a favorite hangout that featured slot machines, seafood, dime hot dogs, and fifteen-cent hamburgers. The most expensive meal in the house was a one-dollar porterhouse steak dinner. The Black Cat also offered the chance to be photographed with grass-skirted hula girls. Kau Kau Korner, a drive-in restaurant at the entrance to Waikiki, featured a much-photographed CROSSROADS OF THE PACIFIC sign, which emphasized the islands' remoteness with directional signs giving mileage to many world cities. At night, the servicemen moved to the city's hotels, bars, and restaurants, which varied from little hamburger dives to Chinatown's Wo Fat restaurant, a first-class establishment near the red–light district.

Cornelia steered clear of all of it, although she did take quickly to the city and its laid-back life. Honolulu was a little bigger than Nashville, with a population of 180,000. There were Piggly Wiggly stores for groceries, and shops throughout Chinatown for rice, herbs, and seasonings. In place of Nashville's Castner-Knott and Cain-Sloan, there were upscale stores like Liberty House and McInerny's.

Cornelia adopted the local custom of including a carnation or other flower in her hair when she dressed up to go out on the town. Otherwise, her wardrobe ran to the casual, and she generally came to work in a jumpsuit or tailored slacks and a sport shirt. "I don't think Cornelia was interested in clothes and things like that," Betty said. "I never saw her in a dress. She was feminine, but she was just a good tomboy kind of a gal."

Ole's hangar was a big Quonset hut held up with metal struts. One of the instructors discovered that it acted like a radio antenna—if you put your ear in the right spot, you could hear one of the Honolulu stations. Sometimes, between flights, Cornelia and Betty would run to a spot along the wall and listen to music.

Ole threw occasional hangar parties at which staff and friends gathered for drinks in the evening. The women learned to keep a wary eye on Cowboy. Normally shy and laconic, impassive behind his high cheekbones and leathered face, he became, after a few drinks, an avid skirt-chaser, asking them to dance and offering to drive them home. In such moments, Cornelia would simply laugh and keep her distance.

"She was secure and had a lot of confidence in herself," Betty said. "She didn't seem to have any hang-ups. She was a good sport, and all the guys, the other instructors, liked her. She had grown up with brothers like I had, and we were both very comfortable around guys in a pal-type relationship."

In Hawaii, men outnumbered women tremendously and it was not uncommon for an attractive young woman like Betty to get invitations for six or seven dates in a single day. There were months at a time when she didn't spend a single evening at home. Cornelia seemed to be focused on other things. "She was tall," Betty said, "which meant more then than it does now, and I don't think she was that interested in dating. She was dedicated to her flying."

There was one exception: Bill McCain, a 6-foot-1-inch navy lieutenant assigned to the cruiser *Indianapolis*. He was one of Cornelia's first students, and the two of them hit it off. Dark-eyed and dark-haired, McCain came from a wealthy background—his father was president of New York's Chase Bank—and he was an intellectual who would much rather discuss books, history, or the navy than go dancing. He and Cornelia saw each other occasionally, and he quickly fell in love with her. Cornelia greatly enjoyed his company, but her feelings were much more platonic. If she was going to fall in love, it would be with someone toward whom she felt more passion than she did for Bill.

Their relationship was played out against a day-to-day existence that was decidedly schizophrenic. Navy destroyers and civilian tourist ships shared the same harbor. The lights would go out as Cornelia read in her apartment late at night. The military remained constantly ready for war with the Japanese—most likely, people assumed, in the western Pacific.

Cornelia allowed few of the harsh realities of island life to show through in her letters home. She knew how concerned her family was, and she knew her mother and Dudley had an especially difficult time with the job she had chosen. Cornelia herself was warned that her mother's frantic social life had not slowed down; she was feeling the twin tugs of her restless independence and her deep roots in Fortland and family. On Friday, November 14, she wrote to Rufus.

Rufus dear,

Your letter was so sweet. It was so like the ones Dad used to write. Yours are the only letters with news of family doings. Mother's are so few & dreadfully far between & so full of her strenuous endeavors that they never fail to distress me. Can't some of you make her slow down? That's the greatest sadness connected with my work—that I am so far away from you all.

As you probably gathered from my letters to Mother, I'm of two minds about Honolulu—it is truly beautiful & such weather as could never be found anywhere—all blue & green & gold, sunshine without that drenching heat you might expect in the semitropics. I spend my one day off prone on the beach (and not Waikiki, that Coney Island of the Pacific), absorbing sun & surf & resting up from my soldier-sailor-defense worker students. For this is really a boom town & that I don't like. Hectic & full of petty & not so petty irritations. I'm glad I came but the islands are not for me. I miss the season changes & the trains that take you places. There is a Toonerville Trolley Train that putters around the island. One of the local proverbs says that when that train begins to look like a train on the mainland, it is time to go home. Already it looks bigger & bigger to me & last midnight I heard it whistle. That peeping little whistle contained all the magic of unknown places—if ever you have read Thomas Wolfe's books & his descriptions of trains & that quality of wonder contained in a smoky line of cars hitched to each other on the rails, you may understand what I mean.

There's so much poetry in so many things—my dearest. I've had so much happiness given me & for all of it I am grateful to everyone who has touched my life & added joy. And so many times a day I'm choked with love & gratitude to Mother & Dad, who made my way of life possible & who gave us our standards of integrity & loyalty & the ability to love life & value wisdom & beauty.

The happiness I have earned for myself is deeply good too. The friends I've known in so many places, the knowledge I've thirsted for & gained & the limitless prospect of more & more, the simple fact of having earned a living for myself with my hands & the skill that they can produce, the deeply satisfying pleasure of flying & the convictions such as they are that I have come to.

And if I leave here I will leave the best job that I can have (unless the national emergency creates a still better one). A

very pleasant atmosphere, a good salary, but [by] far the best
of all are the planes I fly. Big & fast & better suited for
advanced flying. I'm sure that if I ever got a similar job it
would be an accident—as this was a very lucky accident. But I
will be home anyway, maybe just for a visit, but I'm aching
for Fortland & all the beauty of our lives there. And this is not
homesickness entirely—it is the knowledge of what I want.

All love,

Cornelia

The first week of December consisted of the usual work for
Cornelia: flights in the Cadet, the Waco, and other airplanes. On
the sixth, after flights in the Cadet and a Ryan ST, a low-wing
all-metal plane, she had a session in a Hawaiian Airlines Link
Trainer, a flight simulator designed to give her practice in instrument flying.

Then came the fateful morning of the seventh, of which
Cornelia later wrote:

The day had begun for the civilian pilot instructors as
all Sunday mornings began, earlier than usual. For Sundays
were our busiest days with a double rush of students, hopping passengers, and the crowds of Sun. afternooners who
wanted to go "flightseeing" around the island or between the
islands.

As I drove from Waikiki to our airport, which is bounded
by Hickam Field and lies almost directly adjacent to Pearl
Harbor, the early morning sunlight lay quietly on the island;
the stillness of daybreak was everywhere.

When I arrived at 6:30, the grease monkeys were warming up the airplanes, which stood quietly in the flight line. I took off with my regular Sun. morn. student, a defense worker named Suomala, and we began landing & takeoff practice.

The Japanese fighter planes were at that moment approaching the island.

Eleven

The attack on Pearl Harbor crippled the Pacific Fleet. The battleships *Arizona, California,* and *West Virginia* were sunk, the *Oklahoma* was capsized, and the *Maryland, Nevada, Tennessee,* and *Pennsylvania* were heavily damaged. Ten other ships were sunk or severely damaged, more than 140 aircraft were destroyed, and another 80 were damaged. More than 2,000 U.S. military personnel were killed, including several of Cornelia's students and Monty Whitehead, Doris Duke's date for dinner with Cornelia and Betty. On Monday, December 8, Congress declared war on Japan.

Concerned that her family might worry about her, Cornelia tried to send a cable, but the navy was deluged with 350,000 cables, which could be delayed for as long as five days for censorship.

Cornelia called Betty on Monday morning from the airport, and the two met at the field to look over the damage. They walked to the plane Cornelia had been flying during the air strike. It was parked now on the concrete slab between hangars, and they were astounded at the sheer number of hits it had taken. There were holes in the floor on either side of the stick and on the wings. Other bullets had come perilously close to the gas tanks, and there were holes scattered randomly the length of the plane. It was impossible to tell how much damage might have come during the first burst Cornelia heard in the air and how much was due to ground strafing during or after her landing.

For days after the attack, radio stations were silent except for sporadic announcements, including reports that barges crammed with thousands of Japanese troops were landing on the north side of the islands. Cornelia's initial disbelief had turned into an uneasy jumpiness, and she told friends that an alarm two weeks later frightened her more than the attack had. Until they learned to recognize the sounds of different American planes, they cringed at the sound of every overhead engine.

There would be no more flying for Cornelia, Betty, or, indeed, any civilian in Hawaii for the rest of the war. Nonmilitary air traffic was shut down, and most of the private airplanes in the islands were shipped to the mainland and sold.

Overnight, the character of Honolulu changed. Buildings downtown had been heavily damaged by the navy's own anti-aircraft fire. Gas stations were shut down at first, and then gasoline was tightly rationed, as was liquor. People were required to carry gas masks, and the city remained under blackout conditions. Sirens sounded at dusk, and people had to stay where they were at that moment until the all-clear was sounded the next morning.

Each house or business was required to be blacked out at night, so the island's stores quickly ran out of fabric for blackout curtains. "They sold out right after the attack and never could replace them," said Betty, "and there was just so much glass there."

Defense workers walked up and down the streets to ensure compliance. One night, as Betty was lying on the floor of her house, smoking a cigarette, she heard a knock on the glass door. "Put out your cigarette," a defense worker ordered her. "It could be seen from the air."

Many hotels capitalized on the situation by holding dances and selling rooms to patrons so they could stay overnight behind the blacked-out windows. For the most part, though, the carefree aspects of life in Hawaii were gone. Radio stations announced for weeks that the Japanese were expected to return. "I think the consensus was that they would come back and take over the island," Betty said.

People fired their Oriental servants. Many stopped drinking milk, which was home-delivered, often by people of Japanese extraction, after rumors circulated that poison could be injected through the cardboard caps. Travel after dark was permitted only with a pass, and even then there were stops at military checkpoints on every corner. Headlights were covered with blue cellophane except for a small hole in the center that gave just enough light to see straight ahead.

Cornelia found a job taking applications for work supervised by the army engineers. It required, she said, listening to a great deal of pidgin English. She moved out of her Waikiki apartment and moved in with the Andrew family. Because there was nothing else to do, she used the evenings and weekends for reading, but she ached with the desire to fly again. She had amassed 900 hours of flying time in 21 months, and now she was grounded. Determined that she could be doing "something more constructive for my country than knitting socks," she wanted simply to get out of Hawaii.

Leaving now, though, was impossible. Cornelia tried booking passage, but the government had placed a ban on leaving the islands. Finally, Rufus was able to arrange for passage out through his friend, Tennessee Senator K. D. "Fritz" McKellar.

Late in January, as Cornelia waited in Honolulu, a telegram arrived for her at Fortland from Jacqueline Cochran, one of the nation's premier flyers. Cochran had won the Bendix Air Race in 1938, had broken Howard Hughes's speed record for a flight from New York to Miami, and had won several major aviation awards. Encouraged by President and Mrs. Roosevelt to organize the training of women pilots for the Army Air Force, she drew up a plan with the Air Transport Command. It was rejected by General Hap Arnold, but Cochran continued to research the names and records of every licensed female pilot in the country. There were 3,000 with some flying experience, about 250 with commercial licenses, and less than a hundred with more than 500 hours of flying time. The last group, suggested Arnold, might be recruited to ferry planes for the Royal Air Force Air Transport Auxiliary in England. It was a move that would pacify Cochran and offer a chance for service to the women who wanted it.

Cochran sent telegrams to the small group of highly experienced female pilots she had found, and Cornelia was one of them. The telegram assured potential volunteers there would be no women ferrying planes in the United States "for many months." If these women wanted a chance to serve now, she told them, this was it. They would be working under combat conditions, in terrible weather, and without radios, so they would have to be the best.

Even if Cornelia might have welcomed such an opportunity under normal circumstances, it was now out of the question. The contingent was to leave for England around the first of March, and Cornelia could not arrive in the United States until then. Once she got there, she would be only too eager to stay put for a while.

On January 28, a month before she set sail for San Francisco, Cornelia wrote to her mother. She knew the journey could be a perilous one, for it was rumored the Japanese might well attempt to sink commercial shipping.

"I'm filled neither with a feeling of morbidity nor a prescience of disaster," she wrote. "But the ocean voyage I will be making shortly has elements of danger, and if I lose my life before seeing you again, dearest, I wanted to say aloha and send you my love forever and forever."

With the possibility of danger firmly in mind, Cornelia also typed out her will that day.

Jan. 28, 1942

I, Cornelia Clark Fort, being sound of mind and body, do make this my last will and testament.

I am making no attempt to have this will made legal and foolproof. I am trusting that my wishes will be carried out.

As I understand it, I have no jurisdiction over my income from my father's estate and it will revert.

I would appreciate if, after all death taxes are paid, the income of my share of the estate for one year's time plus all cash of which I die possessed with the following exceptions be paid to Sarah Lawrence College for the purpose of, in any way they see fit, providing one, two, three, or however many the aforesaid funds will cover, scholarships for a girl or girls from the South.

For example, if the total sum is $3,000, it may be divided into six $500 scholarships for six years of one scholarship each year. The girl must be from the South, not Southwest (Texas, etc.). This fund is to be known as the Cornelia Fort Scholarship and is in appreciation of the deep and sincere intellectual experience I received while a student.

The scholarships are to be given, if such selection is possible, to southern girls who, possessed of intellectual curiosity and wanderlust, are not possessed of the funds for Sarah Lawrence.

The following exceptions to all cash being delivered to the above are:

1. Any debts are to be paid, including any to my mother, Mrs. R. E. Fort, for any reason at all. She need have no proof of debt for there is none. Any statement of hers in re my use of the car or any reason whatsoever is to be acknowledged as just debt.

2. The care of my dearly beloved dog Kevin, which I trust will be cared for in affection out of respect to me.

My possessions are to be disposed of at the discretion of my mother or brother Rufus. Anything can be sold or given away.

My books and music will be used and appreciated I hope or given where they will.

I have a Savings Acct. at the Nashville Trust Co. and two Defense Bonds which I have mailed to myself in Nashville from Hawaii.

My most earnest request is that, except for the first week, *no one* wear mourning for me.

The above requests are simply that. I would like to think that they carried as much authority as legal requests.

My deepest love and affection to all my family and friends.

Cornelia's earlier ambivalence about Hawaii had been replaced by a love that benefited, no doubt, from the aura nostalgia leant it. She later wrote a friend:

> I had the world's best job & loved it violently & could have had it until I died of old age had not the Japanese come calling. . . . The weather was ideal, the students pleasant, the planes wonderful, the pay exorbitant, the hours delightful. And when work was done there were so many places to play & so many nice people to take me playing. All in all, coupled with the music & flowers, I was exceedingly pleased with life.

Still, she and those around her knew the necessity of leaving. As she said later, "None of the pilots wanted to go but there was no civilian flying in the islands after the attack and we wanted to return to the only thing we knew in the hope we could be of use to our country, and each of us had some score to settle with the Japs, who had brought murder and destruction to the islands."

Cornelia arranged to have her car shipped to San Francisco and wrote her mother again, saying, "The end of my waiting is almost in sight." Late in February, she boarded an ocean liner in a convoy headed to San Francisco.

Cornelia had longed for the opportunity to use her flying to serve her country. The attack on Pearl Harbor would help assure that she would get her chance.

Twelve

On Sunday, March 1, 1942, Cornelia watched from the deck as her ship steamed its last miles toward San Francisco. She and the other passengers cheered wildly as it passed under the Golden Gate Bridge.

"Nothing ever looked so beautiful to me as did the California shoreline as we approached it," she told a reporter. "I swore I'd never leave the United States again." She told another that the first thing on her mind when she stepped off the boat was "a bath in fresh water" followed by a chance "to play with some old college pals," including Sally Lowengart and Emylu Adams.

Cornelia came back a changed woman, possessed of a deep-seated self-assurance, carrying a tale guaranteed to enthrall people. The war was on, and the story of the twenty-two-year-old girl who had dodged bullets fired by the Zeros had preceded her. Offers for interviews poured in. On Tuesday, accompanied by Sally and another friend, Lucretia Houghteling Zook, she met in her hotel room with an Associated Press reporter and photographer to talk about Pearl Harbor. Relaxed and animated, she told her story, making it clear that she was determined to get back into the air. "Miss Fort wants more flying," the AP story said, "'preferably ferrying planes for the Army.'" On her way back to Nashville, Cornelia told the reporter, she planned to visit a few airports.

"'San Francisco simply fascinates me now,' she laughed. 'To see all the lights on—it's unbelievable. But I want to get up in the air again. You know, I've been grounded with all the other civilian pilots since that day.'"

As a postscript, the reporter added, "As if most people wouldn't be content to stay grounded the rest of their lives."

Cornelia told the story again at Lucretia's house, this time to a reporter for the San Francisco *Call-Bulletin*. Papers nationwide reprinted the story and ran photographs of a smiling Cornelia, who "consumed cup after cup" of coffee as she talked. Her tale had drama, but she told it with wit and an occasional light touch. Describing her arrival at the hangar, she told one reporter, "Nobody would believe what I had seen. Then someone ran up and said the airport manager had been killed. My student let out one gasp and disappeared. He never did pay me for that half hour of instruction."

On the morning after her arrival on the mainland, Cornelia called her mother to tell her she had reached the States and would drive across country for a visit in Nashville. With airport stops it would take about ten days, she predicted, and this time there were no questions raised about the propriety of her traveling alone.

Cornelia arrived in a Nashville that had changed as much as she had. The city, like others across the country, had been plunged into the war. At least three Nashville sailors, two white and one black, had been killed in the attack on Pearl Harbor. Wartime rationing of meat, coffee, sugar, and gasoline was in effect, as were price controls, and there were shortages of many goods. There were metal and rubber recycling drives. War maneuvers were under way nearby, with men streaming to military bases in nearby Clarksville and Smyrna. They brought with them the same proliferation of vice the city had experienced during the Civil War, and which Cornelia had already witnessed in Honolulu.

Nashville had been weakened by the Depression, but it was still an economically vibrant city. Its 167,000 citizens—the population had doubled in forty years—were ready to put their efforts toward wartime production. By 1942 many Nashville industries were turning out goods for the military or gearing up to do so. The Du Pont plant turned out parachutes. Nashville Bridge Company built naval vessels. General Shoe Corporation manufactured combat boots, and Werthan Bag Company made sandbags.

Defense contracts poured into a plant opened next to the airport in May 1941 by Consolidated Aircraft Corporation of California for the manufacture of an airplane to be called the Vultee. Around the site, new housing went up for thousands of workers —about a third of them women—who were turning out cockpit panels for the P-38 Lightning fighter plane. Murfreesboro Road, which led from downtown to the airport, was revamped as a four-lane highway.

Against this backdrop of thriving wartime industry, Cornelia reunited joyfully with her family. Her brothers by now had all worked for a thriving National Life, and two of them were in the military. Rufus, National Life's agency secretary, received an army commission as a lieutenant and was in the recruiting office in Atlanta. Garth, assistant medical director for the firm, was also a lieutenant, serving at Camp Forrest. As their father had foreseen, they entered the service as officers because of their VMI backgrounds. Dudley, manager of the firm's Atlanta district, never served in the military.

Cornelia's fame preceded her to Nashville as it had to San Francisco, and she quickly found herself in demand as a speaker. On the evening of Wednesday, March 18, she spoke to members of the Civil Air Patrol. Wearing both her aviator's wings and a carnation over her ear in the Hawaiian style, she offered a first-person narrative of an event her listeners already knew to be a pivotal moment in world history.

According to *The Nashville Tennessean*, Cornelia shared "memories both humorous and horrible," and her repertory of anecdotes was growing. Here she told the story of three small private planes that were, like hers, in the air when the attack came.

"Two were not heard from for days," said the *Tennessean*, paraphrasing her remarks. "Then they were found awash on the shore, terribly riddled with bullet holes. The surviving pilot saw his comrades going down and turned to encounter a Jap plane, which pulled up beside him. The Jap slid back the hood and looked him over. Finally he turned his machine guns on him as he pulled up in a steep climb. The bullets caught the tail of the plane, and he glided to a landing with only one bolt holding the tail assembly onto the fuselage."

She told her story again in chapel at her alma mater, Ward-Belmont, and then at the 1942 Home Office Conference of National Life, and again on WSM radio as part of a broadcast designed to sell war bonds.

Despite the circumstances, she was glad to be home. Still, in an April 2 letter to the newly married Helen Dixon, she wrote, "I know & realize half wistfully that I will probably have to leave again—as flying is my only talent & one which is in great demand now." She remained determined to contribute somehow to the war effort, and she knew her best chance was flying. She had begun visiting the airport soon after her return to Nashville, and she joined the CAP and gave lessons when she could. When she flew now, more people than ever recognized her.

"Those were days when we didn't have many heroes," said Hank Hillin, who was growing up on a farm near Fortland at the time. "My mother was a widow, and she looked up to this woman who had achieved so much. We were in awe of her."

Late in April, Cornelia's old flying instructor, Aubrey Blackburne, drove to Berry Field for a visit while on leave from his post in Albany, Georgia, where he was now a flight commander. He spotted Cornelia sitting on a bench at the corner of a hangar. "She looked up and saw me two or three hundred feet away and she just started jumping up and down," Aubrey recalled. "She covered three-fourths of the distance from where she was to where I was and I walked along the other fourth." Both had always been reserved in their displays of affection, though, and their greeting consisted of a warm handshake and hellos.

Cornelia's Nashville friends were impressed with her new maturity and confidence. She had written her old friend Elizabeth Craig earlier, telling her, "I have really found myself in flying. I have found the thing that I didn't know I'd been searching for all these years." There was no longer any question about her willingness to let her intelligence and knowledge show. More than anything, though, she displayed an easily perceived sense of mission and accomplishment.

Cornelia found herself very popular with several new "beaus," as she called them. She received admiring letters from a couple of former students, and Bill McCain remained an ardent suitor. Yet another, according to her sister, Louise, asked Cornelia that summer to marry him. Cornelia, though, was not ready to make any beau permanent.

The closest she came was with Arthur Clendenon Robertson, a dashing divorcé fifteen years her senior who showed up at Berry Field for flying lessons. "Clen," as everyone called him, could trace his family tree to several of Tennessee's most distinguished early citizens, including Andrew Jackson's law partner. His uncle, Luke Lea, was a United States senator who had helped develop Belle Meade and was later jailed in a Depression-era financial scandal. Clen himself was a Rhodes scholar who, as an undergraduate, had covered the Scopes "monkey trial" in Dayton, Tennessee, for the *Yale Daily News*. He had been a rancher in Wyoming and a real estate developer, and when Cornelia met him he worked for *The Nashville Banner*.

He was dark-haired and "deadly attractive," according to an old girlfriend, who called him "a wonderful talker with a great sense of humor." As his ex-wife once said, "he could charm the birds out of the trees." But Clen was also a drinker. His divorce had been bitter, and he admitted to friends that he had once threatened his wife with a fireplace poker. Some thought his dating pattern amounted to fortune-hunting, and there were parents who were horrified at the thought that their daughters might associate with him. Still, he was generally the perfect gentleman, well liked by many in the community, and he had charm and flair despite his cavalier self-absorption. "There's only one thing I like to hear better than the sound of my own voice," he would say, "and that's the tinkle of ice in a glass."

He and Cornelia were drawn to each other as friends and started dating not long after they met. Clen's previous girlfriend recalled that he tipped his own hand in making the switch. "You know," he said once, as he was kissing the woman good night, "you're just about the right height for kissing." She said she knew at that moment he had gotten more serious about his flight instructor. "I knew he'd been dating Cornelia, and that she was taller than he was, so I knew then that he'd been kissing her too," she said.

All the while, the war had continued to spread. The German army was deep in Russia, and fighting was intense in northern Africa and throughout the Asian Pacific. The United States was spending more than a hundred million dollars a day on the war effort, and the Treasury Department was utilizing celebrities ranging from local politicians to Hollywood stars to raise money. Cornelia was asked to make a war bond movie, a short feature to kick off a series called *Minutemen for Victory,* which would be shown in theaters throughout the country in July and August. In it, she described her Pearl Harbor experience, then made an appeal for the purchase of war savings bonds and stamps to help pay for planes and supplies for the armed forces. Cornelia herself began to buy war bonds, and she would buy them regularly for the rest of her life.

The Treasury Department also asked her to appear at war bond rallies in Ithaca and Syracuse, New York. She visited Washington, D.C., first to talk about the rallies, and stopped by the Washington offices of the Ninety-Nines, the international organization of women pilots, while there.

On her way to Ithaca, she stopped in New York City, where a visit to El Morocco won her a place in the May 21 column of newspaper columnist Leonard Lyons.

> COURAGE: Cornelia Fort, the aviatrix who was a target for Japanese planes while she was flying near Diamond Head on the morning of December 7, visited El Morocco on Monday night. She was presented there to Captain Robinson, commander of the *Marblehead,* who had brought his torpedoed ship safely back across the Pacific. "I admire your courage," Captain Robinson told her. . . . "But yours was so much greater," said Miss Fort. . . . "No," said the navy man. "You were alone."

The rally in Ithaca, scheduled for Saturday, was to be a large outdoor event, but the weather was so bad it was postponed. Cornelia and Treasury Department promotion manager Edward Ingle boarded a plane for the short hop to Syracuse but flew into a cloud bank at 300 feet and were forced to return to Ithaca, where they borrowed a car for the trip.

As Cornelia met with a Syracuse reporter, she displayed the intensity of her desire to get back into the air. She was introduced to two local CPTP instructors, who told her they were awaiting orders to join the Army Air Force and were "anxious to see some action."

"I wish I were a man—just for the duration," she told them, speaking with what the reporter called a "vicious intensity." "I'd give anything to train to be a fighter pilot and then meet up with that Jap again."

"With her air experience and temperament she might realize her wish if women were permitted to fight," the story said, summarizing perfectly both her readiness and her helplessness. Referring to her as a "Nashville, Tenn., Junior Leaguer," the story added,

> So she's doing the next best thing a woman can do, assisting in the nationwide sale of war savings bonds and placing herself at the disposal of government aviation officials for whatever work they want done. When and if women are called to ferry bombers, the slim 6-foot instructor pilot who has been flying two years will be among the first to report. She already has her application on file.

That evening's rally was held in Central High School's Lincoln Hall after threatening skies forced it indoors from Thornden Park. It was designed to honor recently naturalized citizens and to sell war bonds and stamps.

The city's mayor welcomed the 1,800 people in attendance, and Cornelia watched from the rostrum as the keynote speaker, U.S. Treasury Department general counsel Edward H. Foley Jr., said, "Total victory over a stubborn and treacherous foe lies only at the end of a very long and very rough road. It demands total effort from all of us. Democracy undergoes the acid test on the home front, and it is here, perhaps, more than on the field of battle, that the American way of life must prove itself."

Cornelia told the story she had told so many times and noted how, after the attack, scale maps with specific objectives marked on them were found on Japanese flyers shot down by antiaircraft fire. "How much they knew, and how accurate they were," she said, "was revealed by this: They flew over three hangars in a row, two of which were full of planes, the other empty. They bombed only the two occupied ones."

After the talks, 100 Syracuse University students dashed around the auditorium taking pledges and selling bonds to audience members. The crowd contributed more than $46,000.

The tour brought Cornelia to the attention of Clark H. Getts, Inc., the management company that handled musical tours for artists like Paderewski and Rachmaninoff and lecture tours for speakers, including Eleanor Roosevelt. The firm's J. Howard Andrews wrote Cornelia on May 29, asking, "Will you be interested in a limited number of lecture and radio engagements during the coming season? What time would be best for you and what fees would you require?"

Cornelia apparently expressed at least tentative interest, as Getts himself followed up with a letter on June 9. He was no stranger to aviation, and he let Cornelia know it: "We used to manage Amelia Earhart, and Beryl Markham, and we now manage Amy Johnson [an Englishwoman who had flown solo from England to Australia in 1930]—probably all of them will be known to you," he wrote. "We would hope to send you to spots to which we originally sent Amelia Earhart and where we know people to be interested in aviation and adventure."

He discussed the firm's percentage, asked Cornelia for a biographical sketch and potential lecture topics, and expressed hope that an office staffer then undertaking a southern trip might visit her in Nashville soon. Cornelia weighed the offer a while longer, decided she did not want to tie herself to a long lecture schedule, and turned it down. She did not want to talk about flying; she wanted to fly.

Cornelia also turned down an offer from a magazine named *Calling All Girls,* which wanted to use her story as the basis for a "true comic strip."

In August, after spending more time with her family, Cornelia took a vacation swing with her mother and Louise through Nova Scotia. Even there she was the subject of press interest. Calling her a "youthful blonde flyer," the Halifax *Herald* repeated many of the familiar details of Cornelia's story.

As she always did, Cornelia discussed her longing to fly for her country. She realized, though, that her sex was a probable roadblock, as she felt it had been when she sought to become an instructor. The nation may have been at war, but it felt no real need to utilize its women flyers. In a later look back at her flying career, Cornelia discussed that time:

> When I returned . . . women weren't allowed to instruct even in those army primary schools which were being run by civilians. The only thing open, in fact the only way I could fly at all, was to instruct CPT (Civilian Pilot Training) programs.
>
> Any girl who has flown at all grows used to the prejudice of most men pilots, who will trot out any number of reasons why women "can't possibly" be good pilots. We grow so used to it in fact that I seldom think of it and almost never get on the defensive as I did constantly right after I soloed and wanted so desperately to be a good pilot.
>
> I was most fortunate to have good advice given me by the two men responsible both for my flying ability and my love of

flying. The only way to show the disbelievers, the snickering hangar pilots, is to show them. And because the confidence in my flying of those two men—who were excellent pilots—came slowly and surely to be reflected in my flying, I gained early the strength not to care about the others.

So I was unhappy but not angry when I was informed on every side that there would be no women's branch of the ferry command. "Look," they would say, "get in the Civil Air Patrol" (an organization composed of civil pilots which is doing great work in coastal patrol).

This was a splendid thought until I discovered that although women pilots could join they could not be used on "missions." I had taught two CPT programs and wanted to do some other kind of flying, for in variation you gain knowledge and I wanted and still want to be as good a pilot—as skilled, as scientific and knowledgeable a pilot as it is possible for me to be.

I was pleased to note that in trade magazines flying services had now progressed to the stage of enlightenment as to specifically advertise for women instructors.

Aha, thought I, mentally beaming, somewhere some of us must have done a pretty sound job if now instead of condescending to hire women pilots they are actually advertising for them. Then someone punctured that balloon by acidly pointing out that employers having had several men instructors whisked away by the draft wanted a nondraftable female who could finish a program in the specified time.

So I decided to take an instrument course and prepare myself a little better for that apparently far-distant day when women pilots would be allowed to fly again.

Cornelia chose a three-month course working with the Link Trainer in Binghamton, New York. The Link, a flight simulator, was a machine that resembled an enclosed airplane cockpit. It turned and dipped in sync with the pilot's manipulations while an operator outside ran the machine and monitored the student's actions. Cornelia was to be part of the first all-female Link Trainer Operator Class.

Cornelia, her mother, and her sister stopped to visit Mrs. Fort's family in Boston, and Cornelia went on to visit the family of Honolulu beau Bill McCain at their summer home in Locust Valley, Long Island. She passed through New York City on the way to Binghamton and had dinner with her old friend Jack Caldwell, who had taken her into the air for the first time. Cornelia spoke of her intense hope that she could serve the army as a ferry pilot. Jack told her the Link Trainer course was her best bet, since it might lead to a Link instructing job, and she should take that avenue if she wanted any kind of job security. Cornelia, though, was adamant. The Link work would last just until she got a chance to fly for the military.

That chance was not long in coming, and it came on September 6, couched in the flat run-on prose of a telegram. It was, though, quite possibly the most beautiful thing Cornelia had ever read.

FERRYING DIVISION AIR TRANSPORT COMMAND IS ESTAB-
LISHING GROUP OF WOMEN PILOTS FOR DOMESTIC FERRYING
STOP NECESSARY QUALIFICATIONS ARE HIGH SCHOOL
EDUCATION AGE BETWEEN TWENTY ONE AND THIRTY FIVE
COMMERCIAL LICENSE FIVE HUNDRED HOURS TWO HUNDRED

HORSEPOWER RATING STOP ADVISE ACTIVE COMMANDING
OFFICER SECOND FERRYING GROUP FERRYING DIVISION END
AIR TRANSPORT COMMAND NEW CASTLE COUNTY AIRPORT
WILMINGTON DELAWARE IF YOU ARE IMMEDIATELY AVAIL-
ABLE AND CAN REPORT AT ONCE AT WILMINGTON AT YOUR
OWN EXPENSE FOR INTERVIEW AND FLIGHT CHECK STOP
BRING TWO LETTERS RECOMMENDING PROOF OF EDUCATION
AND FLYING TIME STOP BAKER END GEORGE=

THE HEAVENS HAVE OPENED UP AND RAINED BLESSINGS ON ME,
she wired her mother. THE ARMY HAS DECIDED TO LET WOMEN
FERRY SHIPS AND I'M GOING TO BE ONE OF THEM.

Thirteen

If Dr. Fort had been old-fashioned, rigid, and less than enlightened when it came to women, he had nothing on the U.S. Army. The army was generally slow to embrace new ideas, and the notion of women flyers had been a long, tough sell. It had been hard enough getting the military to make flying a priority in the first place.

U.S. military flying had begun as a branch of the Signal Corps and came under the aegis of the army in 1918. World War I brought aviation's first swift advances. The world's most powerful nations ordered more than a billion dollars' worth of airplanes from manufacturing companies, which sprang up everywhere. They demanded ever-faster, heavier planes with the improved control and maneuverability required, first for plane-to-plane dogfights and then for aerial bombardment. By the end of the war, thousands of surplus airplanes were on the market, ready to be picked up by barnstormers eager to make a few quick bucks playing off the glamorous legends of daredevil aces like Eddie Rickenbacker and Baron Manfred von Richtofen, Germany's Red Baron.

Billy Mitchell, an outstanding combat air commander during World War I and a pivotal figure in U.S. aviation, argued vehemently that the United States needed a strong and independent air force. That view was opposed by both the army and the navy, and Mitchell's continued criticism of the military's leadership eventually led to his court-martial. At the time of his death in 1936, the army was still not stressing the use of airplanes.

In June 1941, the Air Corps, as it was called after 1926, became the Army Air Force, an autonomous command within the army. Its head was General Hap Arnold, a 1907 West Point graduate who had received flying instruction in 1911 from Orville Wright and had taken over the Air Corps in 1938.

Women had played only a small background role in military aviation. The Women's Air Reserve had been organized to serve as an emergency Air Corps auxiliary, and there was a Betsy Ross Corps, whose members hoped to serve as "aviation minutemen." In the days before World War II, more than 2,000 women flyers took part in the Civil Air Patrol, but for many of them that was simply not enough.

It had never been easy for women to fly, although it helped to be rich or well-connected. The first woman to fly a plane was, in fact, a baroness named Raymonde de la Roche, whose maiden flight, in France in 1909, covered 350 yards. Blanche Stuart Scott persuaded flight pioneer Glenn Curtiss to teach her to fly in 1910. Harriet Quimby became the first American woman to hold a license and the first woman to fly the English Channel, in 1911. A year later, she fell out of an airplane and died.

Women slowly worked their way into every aspect of flying. Katherine Stinson became the first woman member of the U.S. air mail staff in 1918, and seven years later Ruth Gillette became the first woman to enter a national air race. Following her lead, more women began to enter aviation races. In 1935, Ogontz's own Amelia Earhart, the first woman to take part in the prestigious Bendix Race, finished fifth over a Los Angeles-to-Chicago course. A year later, Louise Thaden became the first woman to win the Bendix.

It was Earhart, of course, who became the first female flyer to gain a hero's status. A military nurse and social worker, Earhart gained instant renown as the first woman to cross the Atlantic by plane. She had only been a passenger, but the feat brought her widespread acclaim. Anxious to prove herself as a pilot, she crossed the Atlantic alone in 1932—when Cornelia was finishing seventh grade—and sealed her place in history. She was an active flyer from then on, seeking new routes and challenges and trying to open aviation to more women, until her disappearance during an attempted 1937 flight around the world.

Women were admitted to the Civilian Pilot Training Program at a rate of one for every ten men, and more than 2,000 women received CPTP training, but with the advent of war in 1941, their participation was stopped altogether. That same year, Amy Johnson disappeared over the Thames estuary while ferrying a plane for the British Air Ministry. Like the other women she flew with, she had been making $900 a year, compared to the men's $1,400.

Cornelia's telegram was proof that women pilots would now get their chance to fly for Uncle Sam. General Arnold was pressing American manufacturers to develop and build planes of every description. They were responding, and now someone was going to have to ferry those planes from the factories to U.S. air bases. The task fell to the Air Transport Command's Ferry Division, whose pilots were already sorely needed for overseas deliveries (many were ferrying planes to England under the Lend-Lease program) or for combat missions. In January, at Jackie Cochran's request, General Arnold had delayed implementation of a program to use female pilots. Cochran was working with the Air Transport Auxiliary in England and did not want to miss the chance to head any program started back at home. By midyear, though, the shortage of pilots was simply too acute to ignore any longer. On June 11, Air Transport Command head General Harold George gave the Ferry Division's new commanding officer, Colonel William Tunner, permission to consider using female pilots.

Helping Tunner prepare guidelines for the pilots' qualifications, training, and use was Nancy Love, a twenty-eight-year-old pilot who worked in the Ferry Division's Baltimore office overseeing routing and scheduling. Her husband, Colonel Bob Love, was the ATC's deputy chief of staff in Washington, and his office was near Tunner's. Tunner, who was hungry for pilots, was impressed with the fact that Nancy flew the sixty miles to and from work each day, and he listened when she insisted there were enough highly qualified women pilots to assemble a squadron for ferrying duty.

A year earlier, as Jackie Cochran was researching the names and qualifications of the nation's female pilots, Nancy Love was doing the same at the urging of Army Air Force planner Colonel Robert Olds. Love had written him in May 1940 to urge the establishment of a women's ferrying group for the AAF. Her list would provide her with the names of the 83 women to whom she sent telegrams, beginning the evening of September 5. General Arnold had given his reluctant approval that afternoon, four days after First Lady Eleanor Roosevelt had strongly endorsed the concept in her newspaper column.

The requirements for Cornelia and the others were even stricter than those for male civilian pilots. As the telegram stated, they had to be between the ages of twenty-one and thirty-five (the army did not want to be dealing with minors or menopause), and each had to have a high school education, 500 logged and certified hours of flight time, a commercial license, and 200-horsepower ratings. According to one of the recruits, there was another unspoken but very real rule: "You had to be a nice girl from a nice family." For that reason, every female flyer had to furnish two letters of recommendation. There were probably only 100 women in the country with the requisite flight hours, and roughly a quarter of those were in England with the British Air Transport Auxiliary.

Once they had met the army's rigorous standards, these women would be trained for thirty to forty-five days and would fly only primary and liaison aircraft (the smallest planes the army had) on domestic routes. They were to be paid $250 per month, plus $6 a day when they were traveling. This was $130 less per month than the men were making, a figure said to reflect the smaller, lighter planes the women would be flying. It was also much less than most women flyers made in civilian life as instructors. The squadron would be headed by Nancy Love, whose job had given her great familiarity with military procedures and with planning, mapping, and assigning ferry routes. Her title would be Director of Women Pilots.

Her flyers were to report to the 2nd Ferrying Group at New Castle Army Air Force Base in Wilmington, Delaware. The base was near several aircraft manufacturers, and its commander, Colonel Robert Baker, said he could provide adequate barracks space. Since New Castle was in the East, ferrying flights would be short and Washington would be able to keep a close eye on a program that was considered highly experimental. The number of women to be included varied from 25 to 50, in part because of factors as mundane as the availability of barracks and toilet facilities. The ferrying group was originally to have been a military unit, with the flyers commissioned as second lieutenants, but that idea was scrapped because existing legislation made no provision for such a move. Colonel Baker and Nancy Love proposed organizing the squadron on a civilian basis instead, and that suggestion was accepted. Nancy would report to Baker, a stern administrator known as "Black Bob" because of his black mustache. The group would be called the Women's Auxiliary Ferrying Squadron, but the name was actually an unofficial designation, since the squadron was a civilian group handled as a separate unit "for purposes of obvious convenience in administration," according to an army memo.

Cornelia wrote a quick letter to Sarah Lawrence's Constance Warren, asking that the school immediately send Mrs. Love proof of her graduation, and caught the train for Wilmington. She had hungered for this moment almost since she had begun flying, and she wanted to be the first to report.

The New Castle Army Air Force Base was on Delaware Bay, about five miles southwest of downtown Wilmington. It had begun life as a county airport, and construction was still under way, which meant that it was generally dust or mud, depending on the weather. Trucks and earth-moving equipment were common sights as the barracks and other buildings rose quickly from what had been cow pasture and cornfield.

Coming straight from the railroad station, Cornelia was met at the gate, set in a high metal fence, by an armed soldier. She showed him her telegram, and he got on the phone in the guardhouse. Moments later she was picked up in a jeep that took her to base headquarters, part of a cluster of buildings up a short hill. Headquarters was a long drab green building with a narrow hallway running down the middle. Cornelia walked down the hall to the second door on the right, where she was met by Nancy's secretary, Miss Cohee, a stout, pleasant young woman. Gray filing cabinets lined one wall in the waiting room, and a bookcase with four shelves stacked with military aviation books and pamphlets sat against another.

For all her quickness to respond to the telegram, Cornelia found she was actually the second to arrive. Betty Gillies, an old friend of Nancy Love's with more than 1,250 hours in the air, had flown down in the family plane from her home in Syosset on Long Island on the morning of Labor Day, September 7.

Base housing for the WAFS was not yet available, so Cornelia checked into the Hotel du Pont in downtown Wilmington and returned to the base. She underwent her initial interview, presenting her logbook and letters of recommendation, and was taken by jeep to the base airport, where an oversized hangar was crowded with planes ranging from small trainers to the biggest bombers. Lieutenant Joseph P. Tracy supplied her with a khaki one-piece summer flight suit, a helmet, goggles, and a 30-pound parachute pack, then walked her to a Fairchild PT-19A, a silver primary trainer with a 165-horsepower engine, for her flight test.

Cornelia knew that her future as a pilot was riding on how she performed in the plane she was about to step into. In a military setting where men were at best skeptical of women's abilities as pilots, an instant's hesitation or inattention could send her packing, ending forever the opportunity to fly for her country.

She strapped on the parachute, climbed into the metal bucket seat in the rear cockpit, and buckled herself in. Tracy took the front cockpit and instructed Cornelia to put on the earphones so he could talk to her throughout the flight. An enlisted man with a hand crank walked along the left wing and began cranking the propeller, Tracy turned the ignition switch as the propeller began to turn, and the engine roared to life. The enlisted man pulled the wheel chocks away, and Tracy guided the plane down the taxi strip. He got the green light from the tower and rolled down the runway and into the air. Rising and turning until they were headed west, he told Cornelia, "The du Ponts have an airstrip a little west of here. We'll head that way for some takeoffs and landings. Now, you take it. Do some forty-five-degree turns and climb some more."

Cornelia took the controls, got herself adjusted to the plane's feel, and started her climbing turns. Tracy had her perform stalls, spins, steep banks, lazy eights, and the high-powered climbing turns known as chandelles. All were maneuvers Cornelia had learned from Aubrey, and she had practiced them over and over in the skies above Nashville. Her deft touch with the plane showed. She performed the maneuvers flawlessly.

The du Pont field was a short grass strip cut into thick Delaware woods, and the base's flyers used it for practice. Cornelia handled the tight descent over the treetops and onto the runway well and effected some landings and takeoffs before flying back to the base.

While Cornelia waited, three officers reviewed her flight log and discussed her flight with Lieutenant Tracy. Finally, they told her she had passed. Cornelia called her mother to tell her the good news, which her mother relayed to the *Tennessean* for a story that appeared the next morning. Quoting Mrs. Fort, the newspaper said, "Cornelia has been trying to get something like this ever since she came back from Hawaii."

ATC Commander General George had hoped President Roosevelt would announce the establishment of the new female squadron, but that chore was ultimately left to General Arnold. On September 10, General George, Colonel Tunner, and Nancy Love met in Arnold's office for the announcement, only to learn that Arnold had been called out of town unexpectedly (and conveniently, some thought). The task fell instead to Secretary of War Henry Stimson, and the group reassembled in his office. There, reporters and photographers took one look at Nancy and knew they had a story. A highly skilled twenty-eight-year-old woman pilot heading up the first group of female flyers ever to be associated with the military, Nancy was an editor's dream. She was beautiful, with hazel eyes and short blond hair prematurely streaked with gray. Press attention from that moment on would be intense, and descriptions would invariably mention, at least in passing, Nancy's attractiveness.

Like Cornelia, Nancy had fallen in love with flying instantly. She was sixteen-year-old Nancy Harkness when she went for her first airplane ride with a barnstormer in her hometown of Houghton, Michigan. She told her parents that night she wanted to quit school and start flying. Her physician father said she could fly but added that she would most certainly remain in school. She had soloed while a student at the Milton Academy in Massachusetts and became the youngest woman in the United States to earn both her private and commercial licenses. She attended Vassar and was suspended for two weeks and grounded for a semester after buzzing the campus during a low-flying joyride.

After her sophomore year, Nancy dropped out and sold airplanes at East Boston Airport, where she met Bob Love, an Army Air Force reserve flying officer who had started his own aviation company. They were married in 1936. Nancy worked as a test pilot, entered an occasional air race, and practiced tight turns flying around Boston Harbor's lighthouses. By 1938 she was working with Bob, overseeing fifty employees, running charters, giving lessons, and selling planes that she often flew to customers. She ferried a number of planes to the Canadian border for eventual delivery to England under the Lend-Lease Act, and that experience had given her the impetus to suggest that women ferry planes in the United States. Now that the WAFS had been set in motion, her combination of talent, experience, and serene beauty made her the perfect poster girl.

Stimson told reporters there would be no more than fifty women in this first unit. He gave Nancy a lengthy introduction and asked her to stand, to "let the ladies and gentlemen have a look at you." She and General George posed for photographs and answered questions before she headed back to Wilmington.

Nancy returned to the base to find her first two recruits—Cornelia and Betty—and another group of reporters and photographers. An Associated Press photo taken that day shows Nancy examining Cornelia's logbook. Nancy, in sandals and a striped civilian dress, was fully four inches shorter than Cornelia, who wore a jumpsuit and saddle oxfords. That photo, like those of Nancy and the general shaking hands, appeared on the front pages of papers all over the country.

Nancy told the press that four weeks' training would begin shortly and talked about the women pilots' qualifications, their pay, and their civilian status—they were officially civil service employees. No doubt in response to the question, "What does your husband think of your appointment?" she told them he thought it was swell. She also told them, "The squadron was formed to release men for more difficult flying jobs." With women ferrying lighter planes, she said, "the men can be used to ferry more complicated aircraft to various points in this country and to war combat zones."

At the time, women flyers in Britain—the ATA girls—were flying more than 140 types of planes, from light trainers to heavy bombers, but bigger planes were just a tantalizing possibility for the WAFS. "If they show they can fly four-engined bombers safely after proper periods of training and preliminary work," said General George, "I see no reason right now why they may not get the chance."

Betty, at thirty-two, was one of perhaps fifteen women in the country licensed to fly multiengine aircraft. As Betty Huyler, whose family owned the Huyler Candy Company, she had begun flying at eighteen because she wanted to share the chief interest of her boyfriend, navy aviator Bud Gillies. She trained for both nursing and flying until she jumped at the chance to work as a flight instructor for Curtiss Aviation. Betty was a charter member and former president (Amelia Earhart had been the first) of the Ninety-Nines, a group of women pilots formed in 1929 when 99 of the 117 licensed women pilots in America met at Long Island's Curtiss Field.

Cornelia revered Betty's and Nancy's years of experience. Still, she had flown three-fourths as many hours as they had in just two and a half years.

Four more women had checked in by the afternoon of September 11. Aline "Pat" Rhonie, another Long Island flyer, had more than 2,600 hours in the air, nearly twice as much time as the others. She had served with the women's Red Cross ambulance corps in France and was part of the British Women's Volunteer Service. Accepted as a ferry pilot by the British, she had decided instead to wait for a chance to fly in the States. Dark-haired and petite, she was also an accomplished painter—and a divorcée, a rarity at the time. Catherine Slocum, another instructor, was heiress to the Luden cough drop fortune and the wife of the general manager of *The Philadelphia Evening Bulletin*. She and her husband had four children and lived close enough that she could commute for a while. (She would eventually return home to care for her children.)

Helen Mary Clark of Englewood, New Jersey, had been flying with the Civil Air Patrol and had a little under 600 hours in the air. A slender, attractive woman with strawberry-blond hair, she grew up next door to Ambassador Dwight Morrow, whose daughter Anne had married Charles Lindbergh. She and her husband, Englewood's mayor, had two sons.

The only one of the first group who did not come from a privileged background was Adela "Del" Scharr. A tall dark-haired policeman's daughter, she was a schoolteacher and CPTP instructor who had taken the train in from St. Louis. Already in her mid-thirties, she had more than 700 hours in the air.

With their quarters not yet ready, these first women took rooms at local hotels, the du Pont or the Darling, or at a nearby guest house called the Kent Manor Inn.

On Saturday, September 12, Cornelia received her photo ID

card and officially undertook her ninety-day appointment as "a civilian pilot employed by the Ferrying Division, Air Transport Command." Two days later, crews from *Life* magazine and from Pathé newsreels, which aired weekly news broadcasts in movie theaters, arrived at the base. Like most of the journalists who would follow, these crews knew something historic was developing.

Nancy, dressed in a custom-tailored gray-green uniform, was joined by Betty, Cornelia, Helen Mary, and Pat, all wearing skirt suits and carrying empty suitcases and purses to re-enact their arrival. Del, who had not yet taken her flight test, stood nearby out of camera range.

On September 16, Colonel Baker assembled the group at base headquarters, where Nancy was sworn in using an oath identical to the one for commissioned officers. He also swore in the WAFS, who now numbered eight since the arrival of new members Esther Nelson and Teresa James.

Esther was a tall brown-haired flyer who had operated a flying school in Ontario, California. Teresa was a petite dark-haired Pittsburgher who had earned a reputation as a show-stealing stunt pilot. A fiery soulmate of the Jersey Ringels of the world, she earned $200 a show with a routine that included a 26-turn spin from two miles up, which she ended by pulling out at 1,000 feet into a series of loops and snap rolls before spellbound crowds. She was, for good measure, another CPTP instructor.

Cornelia and the other WAFS found out their course work was to be more detailed than that given to the male pilots. They would spend four weeks, from 9 A.M. to noon, learning the specifications of planes, paperwork requirements, meteorology, navigation, routing, and airport traffic laws, Morse code, military law, and the courtesies and customs of the service. After lunch, they would gather in the Alert Room, a big rectangular area inside one of the hangars, where they would receive instructions for the afternoon's flying. Weather permitting, they would fly in the planes they would be ferrying, alternating solo work with dual flight checks accompanied by instructors. It galled some of them that the men would go through as little as nine days of training while they would be studying for a month. Cornelia was especially incensed. She and many of the other women had taught the ground school subjects they were now taking; only the military procedures and regulations would be new. Cornelia was facing the kind of uncompromising rigidity she had faced with her father, and she didn't like it any better now that the decision-maker was the army.

"We're not going to go through all that again," she said indignantly. "Why, as flight instructors, we know all that." But Nancy was firm. Not all the WAFS had been flight instructors, and she was determined that the group would display solidarity and go through together whatever training the army had planned. There was simply too much at stake.

Particularly as more women joined them, the WAFS' attitude grew to be one of high-spirited tolerance. They knew they were good pilots, many of them with far more experience than the men now training them. They were also students of the history of flight; at least two had brought copies of Billy Mitchell's biography with them. Sometimes they laughed about the instructors' patronizing attitudes. Teresa, for instance, was among the best flyers on the base, male or female. She had a commercial license and instructors' ratings and had done some of the trickiest flying imaginable.

Nevertheless, her initial flight check noted, "Needs more time on turns."

Cornelia told her mother, "A small example of the mismanagement of our leaders is this—my Link instructor is an enlisted man but he graduated from Harvard Business School and Harvard University; another one was a Professor of Romance Languages at Yale. And some of the officers on the post don't know 'ain't' from 'no how!'"

Still, the women were grateful for the chance to be flying, and they were eager to prove they could do it the military way. Cornelia later wrote:

> We learned the Army traffic pattern, the necessary paperwork for a ship's delivery. You sign a paper at the factory accepting the ship and it's your baby until the receipt is signed at the delivery point. We reviewed navigation and meteorology, both of which all of us had to know in order to be qualified. The qualifications for the first group were high and all of us understood why.

On September 18, the WAFS moved into their new home: Bachelor Officers Quarters 14, chosen when modifications to the intended women's barracks could not be completed in time. BOQ 14 was a two-story 44-room wooden building, painted pea-green and sitting in a treeless field; it had a few tiny shrubs at one end.

The group had been bolstered by four more recruits. Barbara Poole was an accomplished flyer and instructor who had been the nation's youngest licensed pilot when she earned her license at sixteen in 1936. She met all the qualifications except for recent time in larger aircraft, which Nancy sent her off to get, with the understanding that she would hold her place and seniority until she came back. Helen Richards, twenty-one, was a blond Californian who had been a CPTP instructor in Boise, Idaho. Barbara Towne, another California native, had used her allowance to pay for after-school flying lessons and then attended the Ryan School of Aeronautics in San Diego, working alongside the shop mechanics between flights. Newly married, she told the other WAFS she was "not one to spend the war in a community of women knitting." Alma Heflin McCormick was a well-known Piper Aircraft test pilot and author. Like Poole, she was sent for more time with bigger planes. She came back a week later, with the time under her belt, but washed out because so much of her Cub experience did not transfer to the other planes she flew.

Over the next few weeks, a large second group of pilots came in. While most of the original WAFS had been married, this group was largely single. Many were pretty, and they livened up the social life at BOQ 14.

Gertrude Meserve was a twenty-three-year-old Bostonian who had taught hundreds of MIT and Harvard students as a CPTP instructor. Florene Miller, twenty-one, was a dark-haired beauty from Texas who learned to fly after her second year at Baylor and had taught classes "morning, noon, and night" before she got to Wilmington. Even in a group which included several very attractive women, she stood out. Her irresistibility when it came to male flyers led Nancy Love to refer to her as "Flypaper."

Evelyn Sharp was a barnstormer and instructor from Nebraska with nearly 3,000 hours in the air. Nancy Batson had seen the announcement of Nancy Love's appointment as head of the WAFS in a paper in Miami, where she was a flight instructor. She quit her job, drove home to Birmingham, Alabama, bought some new clothes, got a letter of recommendation from the manager of the local airport, and headed for Delaware. She arrived unannounced, wearing a herringbone tweed suit with a hat, gloves, and matching alligator bag and shoes.

B.J. Erickson was a dark-haired twenty-two-year-old from Seattle who had transferred her students in the WTS (the navy version of the CPT) to another instructor in mid-course after receiving her invitation to join the WAFS. She drove to her parents' home to say goodbye and pick up her clothes and then bought her first train ticket for the long ride to Wilmington. Phyllis Burchfield's father was one of Pennsylvania's pioneer oilmen, and his 3,000 acres adjoined the Drake property on which oil was first discovered in Titusville. An animal lover and expert equestrian, she was a twenty-nine-year-old CPT instructor with 1,700 hours.

Delphine Bohn was a petite, personable Texan and one of the few newcomers to smoke and drink, as most of the first eight WAFS did. Esther Manning was a pretty brunette from a wealthy upstate New York dairy family. Barbara Donahue, a tall black-haired heiress to the Woolworth fortune, walked into the barracks carrying a leopard-skin coat.

After moving in to the BOQ, the WAFS went to the sub-depot for their flight equipment—green army coveralls, leather jackets, helmets, goggles, sunglasses, traveling bags, and parachutes. They would get their fur-lined winter flying suits later. Nothing had been designed with women in mind, and the tinier WAFS, like five-foot-one-inch Betty, swam in their outfits. The cuffs of even the smallest flight suits had to be rolled up. Cornelia had the opposite problem. At six foot, she was, as usual, taller than many of the men around her, and her first flying suit rode an inch or two above her ankles.

The new WAFS were called "the cream of the country's aviatrixes," and they were, to be sure, an elite group; hundreds of women would seek unsuccessfully to join. Still, it wasn't just their accomplishments in the air that drew attention.

"This first group," said an article in *Flying* magazine that December, "has more than an average share of charm and glamour as well as aviation experience." Photos of the women in a variety of settings were appearing in newspapers and magazines nationwide.

The WAFS found that making themselves at home in BOQ 14 would be a real challenge. The rooms, for which each of them paid $4.50 a week, were primitive, with exposed vertical two-by-four pine wall studs and plenty of gaps between them for wind and weather to get through. Each room had an iron cot with a sagging mattress and an army blanket, a maple chest of drawers, bright blue scatter rugs, and a large portable pine wardrobe. Near the window end of each room, under a shelf four feet off the floor, was a metal bar on which they could hang their clothes.

The WAFS were told to make their beds the army way. Betty, who had both nurses' training and Ogontz's military rigors in her background, lent her expertise, teaching the others and bouncing quarters off the blankets to test their tightness.

None of the barracks had curtains or blinds. That didn't matter when there were only men on the base, but the women had to dress and undress in the dark or in the hallway. Soon, in deference to them, each room was equipped with venetian blinds, a dressing table, and a wall mirror. A few WAFS went to the first floor's empty rooms and got second mattresses to try to improve their cots. Still, Delphine Bohn later remembered "flesh indented with Picasso designs developed by metal cots, thin mattresses, and too-thin silk nighties . . . soon exchanged for high-neck flannel pajamas."

By the end of the month, the rooms had been given as many personal touches as the women could muster. "Most of the rooms," said a September 26 *New York Times* article, "have already been frilled up with feminine touches. Quilted bedspreads, cretonne curtains, whatnots and knitting bags have made their debut in these hitherto masculine quarters. Pictures of husbands, sweethearts and children cover bureau tops. A stuffed toy penguin stands guard in one corner. And books, covering a wide variety of tastes, have been placed on wooden ledges halfway up wooden walls."

Cornelia's room was even smaller than her tiny bedroom at home. If there was one thing it would have quickly, though, it was books. Cornelia kept up her reading as best she could despite the hectic pace of her new life. She was a member of the Book-of-the-Month Club, and she sent and received packages of books regularly, swapping with her mother and friends as she read them. She also lent books to the other WAFS. Writing would remain important to her as well. She continued to write regularly in her diary, and she kept up correspondence on a number of fronts. Her letters to her mother contained monthly checks of $25 for rent on her tiny room at Fortland; in keeping with her father's notions of responsibility and self-support, she had been making these payments ever since she had begun working. Like most of the WAFS, she often requested both necessities and the occasional luxury. Early on, she wrote to her mother:

Thanks for the bottles etc. How about the flashlight, the
Old Spice Bath Powder (in a brown round tube for traveling
in or on my bureau) and my jodhpur boots. I'm sending
home some clothes; if you will have the yellow coat cleaned
I'll reimburse you. Do you have any idea what the cost of all
your express and postal charges to me are? Also the horn-
rimmed dark glasses in left drawer of study bookcase.

Hope to get a glimpse of you soon. I love you—

Cornelia

Along with the doilies and photos and other personal touches,
Cornelia was quick to install an in-room wet bar, setting up liquor bottles atop the dresser. Some of the others had brought
bottles as well. Betty always had a Cuba libre before dinner, and
she, Cornelia, and Nancy often ended the day with a drink in one
of their rooms. There was a relaxed camaraderie about this quickly
established tradition. Sometimes after dinner there would be sessions of "hangar flying" (flying stories, tall and otherwise), gossip,
and reports on the current status and future plans of the WAFS.
"The choicest news," Del said later, "was often told when the
persons in attendance sat with drinks in their hands."

The women at the west end of the second floor came to call
the eastern end the du Pont Lounge because it was dominated by
the eastern finishing-school girls. This was where Cornelia spent
most of her time. It was the spot for the quiet cocktail before dinner and for relatively subdued conversation. The other women
congregated in a loose group that had Teresa James, with her plain-
spoken enthusiasm and strong Pittsburgh accent, as its hub. Her
room, which she quickly furnished with some throw rugs and a

chaise longue and radio her mother brought her, became known as the Waldorf-Astoria.

Sizing up Cornelia and her friends, Teresa was heard to gasp, "My Gawd, did you ever think we'd be with such classy dames?" Teresa was a natural and animated storyteller who would address a sister WAFS as "kid" or "sister" or "you old bag" in an offhand and affectionate way. She could make the others laugh all the way through a long narrative. Having once been in a dance marathon, she took to organizing impromptu dance parties. "Do you old bags know how to boogie-woogie?" she would ask. "Let's go out in the hall and I'll show you how to shag." Evelyn Sharp, a brown-haired live wire who matched Teresa step for step when it came to vitality, would add to the fracas, walking on her hands or turning a somersault. The group would sing songs and swap stories about flying, stopping occasionally for a walk to the watercooler or the nickel soft-drink machine down the hall. Cornelia would sometimes stop in the hall or in a doorway, usually with a book in her hand, to observe, but she seldom joined in. She was neither a dancer nor uninhibited enough to join such boisterous merriment. Often she spent her spare time making detailed entries in her diary, fashioning a running narrative of her life as a flyer.

There were times, however, when the two groups mixed. According to Teresa, "The du Pont Lounge kids came around to us sometimes. They liked a little excitement now and then too."

The mix of gentility and spunk could sometimes make for interesting dynamics. "We were in Cornelia's room one night," said Teresa, "and we were all sitting around yakking, telling flying stories, and somehow we got to where everybody was telling where they went to school. I think it started with Rhonie talking about how she went to Vassar." Most of the group—Cornelia, Betty, Nancy—had gone to finishing schools and major eastern colleges, and Teresa decided she wasn't about to be one-upped.

"Where did you go to school?" Pat asked her.

"I went to Thornhill in Pittsburgh," said Teresa, watching Pat nod as though she knew what a good school it was. "It's one of the best schools in the world," she added. "You really had to do something special to get in."

When the group split up, Teresa took Gertie Meserve into her confidence. "I wasn't gonna let them get away with that," Teresa said. "I never went any further than high school. You know what Thornhill is? It's a correctional school for boys." That evening's brag night would become another one of Teresa's long and uproarious stories.

The WAFS, being mostly young and vigorous, had energy to burn. They hung a dartboard in an unused room at the barracks and used it to relieve tension. They also indulged in their share of practical jokes. Sometimes one of the WAFS would come in at night, push her door open, and find herself doused with the contents of a water bucket that had been balanced atop her door. Pulling the string for the light bulb in the middle of the room might lead to a glassful of water emptying onto her head. Someone might spread Limburger cheese on a radiator, tie knots in stockings or pajamas, short-sheet a bed, or hide oranges between the mattresses.

There was much about BOQ 14 that would take getting used to. The large bathroom featured toilets and shower stalls without doors, but the women had that changed right away. There was also a line of urinals, which many of them had never seen before.

They adapted as best they could. Most mornings, at the sinks and mirrors, according to Del, the women would be "scrambling about, getting in each other's way."

There were two phones in the building, one upstairs and one downstairs, and they began ringing the minute the WAFS moved in. There were over 10,000 men on the base, and these women were young, fit, and in some cases very attractive. They were forbidden to fraternize with enlisted men, but even the officers—and there were a great many handsome young lieutenants and captains—outnumbered them by a huge margin.

Since many of the first group of WAFS were married, they were not interested in the men on base anyway, except for conversation and the occasional dance. Cornelia attracted little attention, Del recalled, since she "looked older than her years. . . . She had a look of austere bookishness, and her long, handsome face did not correspond to the pretty-pretty face so beloved by moviegoers of that era."

Even among the other WAFS, Cornelia's bookishness and occasional standoffishness made her an enigma. Sometimes she was quite sociable, but at other times she was mysteriously remote; she would always be considered by some to be a little aloof. A prime source of mystery was her behavior at breakfast. The WAFS rose at six-fifteen, jostled for position in the bathroom, and then headed—often splashing through rain and mud—for the officers' mess for breakfast.

The mess, like much of the base, had a makeshift feel. *The New York Times* said it looked "more like a summer camp dining room than anything else. Long wooden tables with attached benches occupy the center of the room with an old-fashioned potbelly coal-burning stove at each end. The WAFS, officers, and visiting civilians give their orders for simple, wholesome food to an enlisted soldier-waiter." They paid a cashier for each meal.

The WAFS generally straggled in in twos or threes, sometimes gathering in one area, an island of femininity in a sea of male officers; sometimes they joined a few of the men. In either case, Cornelia would come in, usually after the others were seated, bypass the WAFS, and walk between the two rows of tables to sit in the back by herself. The WAFS watched this for a while, wondering why it was that this pleasant, albeit reserved, southern girl wanted nothing to do with them at the breakfast table. Finally, Florene was appointed to approach her.

"You know," she said to Cornelia one morning, "we'd love for you to sit with us in the morning. And if not, we'd love to know how come. Why do you choose to sit here alone?"

Cornelia, who was simply a slow starter in the morning, looked up groggily, paused, and said, "I just can't stand to have a straight-up egg looking me in the face first thing in the morning, and I'm not going to sit with anybody that's eating them for breakfast."

In the interest of decorum and appearances, the base assigned the WAFS a housemother, an older woman named Mrs. Anderson who quickly came to be called "Andy." It did not seem to matter that there were many wives and mothers in the group, some in their thirties, and that such a setup for male civilians would be unthinkable. Nevertheless, Andy came to be greatly appreciated. When the group began to be dispersed on ferrying missions, she was a constant presence in the barracks at night and would help the women with laundry and other small chores.

On September 21, the WAFS received their first memorandum from Colonel Baker, under the heading GENERAL REGULATIONS:

1. There will be no distinction between male and female Civilian Pilots. They will all be designated Civilian Pilots.
2. Civilian Pilots will have all the privileges of officers, including the use of Officers Club and Officers Mess. Officers Mess hours are as follows: Breakfast, 6:30–8:00; Lunch 11:30–1:00; Dinner 5:30–6:30.
3. Civilian Pilots will stand formation and roll call at 8:00 A.M. each morning.
4. Members of the WAFS will wear summer flying suits during schooling period.
5. Members of the WAFS will live in BOQ #14 during schooling period.
6. Members of the WAFS will not smoke in HQ building during office hours.

The first point was not entirely accurate. Besides the pay differential, the male civilian pilots who qualified would be commissioned as officers after ninety days. The women were never commissioned.

The other big difference between men and women remained the press interest in the latter. Late in September, the WAFS posed for another round of photos, this time for *The New York Times, Cosmopolitan,* the newsreels, and other publications. Eight of them lined up in their overalls, chin straps hanging, goggles perched atop their heads. The feeling of uniformity was broken only by a look at their feet. Cornelia was wearing black-and-white saddle oxfords.

Catherine wore tennis shoes. The mix of styles would last until they bought their uniforms.

The photographers took individual and small-group photos and had the entire crew carry their parachute bags past a row of PT-19s behind a uniformed Nancy. Each stopped at a plane and got in and out for the cameras. Some of the reporters were feature writers with little aviation experience, and one, upon being told what the plane's hatch was, said, "Oh, you mean the lid."

Nancy disliked the publicity, which she considered an intrusion on the work she and the other WAFS were doing. Still, she was expected to pose like the others. From the beginning, Nancy stressed to reporters that the WAFS were experienced pilots undertaking often grueling missions, and she urged them not to play up the supposed glamour. Certainly there was nothing glamorous about her own situation. She had the same kind of desk as her secretary, and when reporters asked for tours of the WAFS quarters, Nancy came out from behind the desk and conducted them herself. Reporters were used to squadron commanders who delegated enlisted men or junior officers to handle such mundane chores.

Nancy's own beauty, though, worked against her desire to maintain a low profile. On September 27, a close-up of Nancy, whose face could only be described as beautiful, looking out from a cockpit, appeared on the cover of *The New York Times Magazine*. It helped establish that image for her. She would soon be featured with a full-page shot in *Life* and would later be named one of the six American women in public life with the Most Beautiful Legs.

Whatever tangential paths the press or public might wander

onto, the women never for a moment lost sight of their mission. They realized at once the weight that was on their shoulders, and they cherished the opportunity too much to let it drop. According to General George, their squadron had been established for the purpose of "determining the suitability of utilizing women pilots in the delivery of military aircraft." Cornelia would later write:

> Because there were and are so many disbelievers in women pilots, especially in their place in the Army, officials wanted the best possible qualifications to go with the first experimental group. All of us realized what a spot we were on. We had to deliver the goods or else. Or else there wouldn't ever be another chance for women pilots in any part of the service.

Teamwork and loyalty would be essential. But for Cornelia, as for most of the others, Nancy was the group's focal point. "No better choice could have been made. First, and most important, she is a good pilot, has tremendous enthusiasm and belief in women pilots, and did a wonderful job in helping us to be accepted on an equal status with the men."

Nancy's personal charm won her as many points as her professionalism did. She carried herself with a cool grace, and she was a hit in the officers' club. Often she could be seen with a group of male pilots around her as she talked about flying and the new program.

The officers' club was a new structure—its grand opening wouldn't take place until October 26—separated from BOQ 14 by an officers' barracks. Although it was open for only an hour or so a day at first, it quickly became the base's social hub. Every day at 5 P.M. the club began to attract officers and WAFS, who would have drinks before walking across the street for dinner at the officers' mess. Groups of men and women would be talking at tables or drinking at the bar, while others played cards or Ping-Pong. The jukebox got a good deal of use, and someone would occasionally play the piano for sing-alongs. Even Cornelia, said Teresa, would "stand there and warble a couple of notes" now and then. Soon there were Sunday-night buffets and twice-a-month dances with live bands. As the weather cooled, a big fireplace piled high with wood gave the place a welcome warmth.

Couples or groups might walk from the club to the base theater, which opened on September 24 and showed first-run movies at 6:30 and 8:30 P.M. four nights a week for 15 cents. That year, *Holiday Inn,* with Bing Crosby singing "White Christmas," was one of the highlights. Otherwise, groups of officers might ask any number of the WAFS to accompany them in cars to the Hotel du Pont for drinks and dancing.

For all the socializing on the ground, fraternization in the air between men and women was quickly forbidden. Bomber pilots had begun offering rides to the WAFS, and the AAF, highly conscious of the press attention the women were receiving, wanted to nip in the bud anything that might suggest the possibility of scandal.

Apparently, Nancy agreed. According to a history prepared by the ATC, "Mrs. Love herself was in favor of most of these stringent regulations. They were simply an attempt to forestall any possible criticism by scandalmongers of the morals of the WAFS. The best proof of the wisdom of this policy is seen in the fact that not once did a report of any laxity on the part of a WAF ever reach the press."

Still, the pilots were conscious of the sexual tension that existed, even if they didn't act on it. That fact was evident even at the breakfast table. Many of the WAFS were coffee drinkers; only a few, in fact, regularly drank tea or milk. That changed drastically when the rumor circulated that the army was putting saltpeter in the coffee to help reduce the sexual urges of the troops, something the navy was reputed to do. Not until the rumor had been dispelled did coffee again became the most popular morning beverage.

On October 15, Colonel Baker forbade male–female joyrides and warned that "under no circumstances will the WAFS endeavor to secure rides on the return trip from any Army Air Base or station." Something male pilots took for granted—the ability to catch a lift on a military plane to get home after a ferrying mission—was off-limits for the WAFS. They were to come back to base from ferrying runs by commercial airline or train, which often meant long journeys from out-of-the-way locations. The only exceptions were flights furnished by group headquarters specifically to take ferry pilots back to the base—flights via what the pilots called Snafu Airlines.

Nancy also announced early that WAFS were not to fly as part of the same flight plan as male pilots. "In going cross-country," Del remembered her saying, "even though their flight is going your way, avoid them."

"Why is that?" Cornelia asked her.

"All the cadets have had flight training in close formation," Nancy answered. "They may be tempted to fly on your wing and horse around. It's against Civil Air Regulations, but they get by with it when they can. We haven't had the training, and as civilians we must not get closer to any other airplane than five hundred feet."

The WAFS were not part of the military, but they were trained as if they were. It was a mixed blessing. They could, for instance, use the officers' club, but they soon found that they were also expected to march. They were unsure how that skill related to their job, but they were, as with everything else, determined to do it right. "All eyes were upon us," Del said later. "We were curiosities, of course, and we easily guessed that inside the nearby administration building onlookers peeked out at us with some amusement, garnering tidbits to relate about our stupidity. The day would come when we would join the men for inspection and parade. They were going to admire us or else!" They marched from eight to nine every morning on the grounds, with Lieutenant Jordan stopping the little troop whenever a member flubbed a drill, calling her name, and taking her to the side, where she would watch the maneuver performed by the others.

After a week's practice, the squadron was hardly a model of precision. The clumsier women, though, were willing to practice, and Betty, who had been an Ogontz drill instructor, became the tutor for the weaker WAFS, marching them up and down the hall at BOQ 14.

Nancy had neither the temperament nor the voice to lead this ragtag group of marchers, but she had to do it. On one early occasion, the group was marching down an unused runway directly toward a ten-foot dropoff, waiting for her to command them to stop or turn or do something. Her mind had gone blank, though, and no order was forthcoming. Finally, the group began to pile up at the edge and spill over onto the embankment. Nancy finally thought to yell "Stop!" and they all fell out, laughing hysterically. Even the normally restrained Cornelia howled.

At last, though, they were marching consistently and well, and on Saturday, October 3, they dressed in their new uniforms, spent a few extra moments with their makeup, and joined Nancy outside the BOQ.

"Are you sure you know how to march?" she asked them. They nodded vigorously, and she laughed. "Well, I don't know how to lead you. Whatever I don't say, you do it anyway."

The WAFS had, they assured her, a good deal of practice at that, and they went off to become part of the 8 A.M. inspection and parade for the first time.

Cornelia would later write:

> For all the girls in the WAFS, I think the most concrete moment of happiness came at our first review. It was a routine weekly inspection, so there was no band and no flag waving, but there was a backdrop of airplanes—hundreds of bombers parked neatly, awaiting foreign delivery. It was a quiet form of drama, but suddenly and for the first time we felt a part of something larger. Because of our uniforms, which we had earned, we were marching with the men, marching with all the freedom-loving people in the world.
>
> And then while we were at attention a bomber took off, followed by four pursuit planes. We knew the bomber was headed across the ocean and that the fighters were to escort it part of the way. As they circled over us I could hardly see them

Fortland, with cattle grazing on a portion of its fourteen-acre front lawn. *Photograph courtesy of Charles Kinle.*

The fearless young rider on one of Fortland's many ponies. *Photograph courtesy of the Fort family.*

Cornelia with, clockwise from top left, Dudley, Dr. Fort, Rufus, and Garth. *Photograph courtesy of the Fort family.*

A photo taken at a family retreat in Sewanee, Tennessee, on
June 3, 1936, when Cornelia was seventeen. From left, Garth,
Cornelia, Dr. Fort, Louise, Rufus, Mrs. Fort, and Dudley.
Photograph courtesy of the Fort family.

The new members of Nashville's elite Cotillion Club, 1939. Cornelia is third from left in the back row. Her friend, Elizabeth Craig, is at left, front. *Photograph courtesy of Elizabeth Porter.*

Cornelia in the studio of Nashville's WSM in the spring of 1942. She was recording an account of her Pearl Harbor experience as part of a campaign to sell war bonds. *Photograph courtesy of the Fort family.*

September, 1942. The last stroll past press cameras at New Castle
Army Airforce Base, Delaware. From left, Teresa James, Cornelia,
Esther Nelson, Betty H. Gillies, Aline Rhonie, Helen Mary Clark,
Nancy Love, and Catherine Slocum. Adela Scharr is hidden behind
Rhonie. *Photograph courtesy of the Fort family.*

In the new dress attire of the unit, Mrs. Nancy H. Love (left), commander of the Women's Auxiliary Ferry Squadron, greets the first four
arrivals at the training base outside Wilmington, Delaware. Left to
right: Cornelia Fort, Helen Mary Clark, Aline Rhonie, Betty H.
Gillies. The photo, taken September 22, 1942, was actually a recreation
for the press. The recruits were in fact holding empty luggage.

Photograph courtesy of the Fort family.

The last WAFS assigned to Long Beach Army Airfield pose with a BT-13, one of the planes they ferried regularly from California to bases all over the South and Southwest. From left, Barbara Towne, Cornelia, Evelyn Sharp, Barbara Jane Erickson, and Bernice Batten. The photo was taken less than two weeks before Cornelia's death.

Photograph courtesy of the Fort family.

for the tears in my eyes. It was striking symbolism, and I think all of us felt it. As long as our planes flew overhead, the skies of America were free and that's what all of us everywhere are fighting for. And that we, in a very small way, are being allowed to help keep that sky free is the most beautiful thing I've ever known.

Cornelia's account did not tell the whole story. The event was a long one, conducted in the glare of a hot sun, and the WAFS, keyed up for the event, were wearing their woolen gabardine flight suits. As visiting officers inspected the assembled troops, Cornelia crumpled slowly to the ground. The others, knowing all eyes were upon them, wanted to help her but were afraid to move. Finally, Cornelia began to come around and, as the assembly was dismissed, the women helped her to her feet.

Colonel Baker came to the barracks afterward, and the WAFS held their breaths as he spoke. He praised them for their performance, saying he hadn't seen a single mistake.

"But what's this I heard about someone fainting?" In the face of their shamed silence, he smiled. "Even West Point cadets have been known to faint while standing at parade rest," he said. "I think they forget to breathe."

The WAFS exhaled, and the episode was soon forgotten.

The weekly parades became a regular part of the squadron's life, so Nancy Love wanted her pilots to take them seriously. One Saturday morning just before eight, Nancy Batson told Love she had a cold and felt too bad to go out and march. Love, however, who had heard Batson and the others coming in at midnight from an evening at the Hotel du Pont, informed her that if she could dance, she could march.

Army policy concerning the WAFS' new uniforms was emblematic of the way the military viewed them. The squadron had received orders early on that they were to wear "standardized attire for recognition purposes," but the directive was not accompanied by funds. The women had spent their own money getting to the base, and now it would be up to them to provide their own uniforms.

Nancy Love had had her uniform made soon after the first WAFS arrived. Since Carlson's, a Wilmington tailor shop, handled the men's uniforms, Nancy had approached its owner, John Carlson, about uniforms for the women. The only material he had in any quantity was a gray-green wool serge, so that's what he planned to use. He worked up a sample, which looked terrible and fit the same way. But Nancy made some changes during her refitting, and soon she was wearing a short gray-green gabardine jacket with lighter slacks and a detached belt—the uniform she wore for the press. Her silver wings and the insignia of the Air Transport Command, provided later, added to the military look.

Now it was time for the rest of the WAFS to get uniforms, and they went as a group to be measured. There are two versions of how Carlson, used to dealing with men, handled the delicate task of measuring inseams.

Teresa James remembered him as shy. "Mr. Carlson was on his knees doing the measuring," she said, "and when it came to the inseam, he would only bring the tape up so far, and then he guessed."

Del Scharr recalled no such timidity.

"The tailor," she said later, "nonchalantly placed the end of the cloth tape up in my crotch and slipped his hand along the tape—and my leg—to the ankle. Later I said to Esther [Nelson], 'He was getting a little fresh, wasn't he?'"

Whatever his approach, the results were consistent. Almost nobody's uniform fit. "The pants were much too long and they bagged in the back," said Teresa. "You could have put a sack of flour in the seat."

The women went back for refittings, adamant that they were going to get their money's worth. Two sets of uniforms, each with skirt and slacks, along with a gray wool overcoat with an extra button-in lining, would set each member of the WAFS back $225, the better part of a month's pay. There would also be Manhattan khaki cotton shirts, white silk shirts for dress wear, an overseas cap, brown oxfords with Cuban heels, white gloves, and a brown leather purse with shoulder strap. The only consolation for the poorer WAFS, like Del, was that Carlson gave them some time to pay. Cornelia took advantage of the installment payments too.

When they finally picked the uniforms up, Nancy Batson left Carlson's and slipped into a photography studio down the street, anxious to have a photo to send home. Soon others followed her, laughing at their mix of pride and vanity as they spotted the others.

Nancy thought her photo turned out beautifully, and she sent copies home. Apparently the photographer thought so too. Soon afterward, as Nancy took a bus into Wilmington, she saw her photo on a large inside-the-bus poster advertising the photographer. Not sure whether to feel flattered or duped, Nancy called him and had it removed.

The uniforms would be complete with the addition of the silver wings of the Ferry Command's civilian pilots above the left breast pocket, Air Transport Command roundels on the shoulder straps, and the insignia of the Army Air Force (a blue circle with yellow wings and a white star with a red center) on the left sleeve with the acronym WAFS stitched below it in blue.

The move toward a more professional look led Nancy Love to tell a greatly disappointed Teresa to cut her thick black shoulder-length hair, saying it would needlessly emphasize her femininity in this man's world and would be a problem to keep neat in windy open cockpits.

Winter flying outfits—"monkey suits"—were issued to the WAFS during the week of October 5. They consisted of bulky leather jackets and pants, leather helmets with chin straps, and face masks, boots, and gloves, all lined to some extent with fur or wool. When winter came, with the women flying open-cockpit planes in frigid, windy conditions, the outfits would be worn over woolen underwear and heavy wool stockings. The suits would also serve a more mundane use. Both the boilers and the plumbing went out on occasion in the BOQs, and there were times when, with no heat and no hot water, the WAFS wore their bulky winter gear to bed.

The same week they got their monkey suits, the WAFS were given cross-country flight checks, traveling in small groups to fields in Hagerstown, Maryland, and Middletown, Pennsylvania. Those fields, like many near the coast during the war, were camouflaged because of their potential as targets for enemy aircraft.

The time for their first mission was approaching, and the WAFS were given the weekend of October 10–11 off. They headed in several directions and then returned to undergo complete pre-mission physicals. A group of doctors examined them in rotation, measuring their height, weight, and blood pressure, giving them hearing, eye, and balance tests, as well as chest X rays, and checking them for everything from flat feet to hemorrhoids.

As was the case in many situations at the base, not all the medical personnel had been prepared for the encounter. Cornelia wrote, "As we trooped into the flight surgeon's office, the tech sgt, who had been medically trained in Texas, said, with eyes popping, 'They never taught me anything about this at Randolph Field.'"

The pilots and other officers continued to have mixed reactions to the WAFS' presence. Some were vocal in their opposition to the idea of women flying, period. Others were cautiously grateful for this new group, knowing they would be able to move up to bigger planes now that women were flying the small ones. In either case, the women knew as their first flight neared that they were under close scrutiny.

The pressure drew them closer together. Cornelia developed a tight friendship with Nancy Love, Betty, and Helen Mary, and some combination of the four of them would often go into town for an afternoon or evening. Cornelia invited Del to lunch at McCafferty's Oyster House in town one autumn afternoon. They ate oyster stew and chatted, surrounded by local workers on their lunch hour.

Cornelia and Del took occasional long walks, which must have re-created for Cornelia some of the feel of Fortland. As the air turned crisp and the leaves began to change, they would cross the base toward the subdepot, wandering through fields and nearby woods to look at plants and birds. Cornelia told Del her Pearl Harbor story on one of these walks. Mrs. Fort, like Dudley, was concerned that Cornelia maintain her spiritual life. Cornelia told Del how her mother, who had not wanted her to fly in the first place, was especially concerned that Cornelia not violate the Sabbath.

"My mother would never have consented to my flying on a Sunday," Cornelia explained. "I couldn't tell her that my job required me to fly on the day of rest. But I got caught that one time [at Pearl Harbor], and she found out that I hadn't been keeping the Sabbath as I should." Faced now with more Sunday duty, Cornelia would deal with the subject the way she had dealt with her smoking. "I just don't tell her about it," she told Del.

The two of them stopped in a marsh one day to pick some cattails to take back to the barracks. As they walked back to the base, every now and then an officer or two in a passing car would stop and lean out, offering them a ride.

"No," Del or Cornelia would say, "we want to walk." Finally, though, two enlisted men in fatigues came by in a jeep, and Cornelia and Del, whose sole exposure to the vehicles had been their first-day rides from the gate to Nancy's office, couldn't help themselves.

"Thanks, yes, we'll be glad to," said Cornelia. They climbed into the back seat and squinted against the onrushing wind as they were taken back to BOQ 14. On the way inside, walking across planks that had been laid over the worst of the mud outside the building, Cornelia turned to Del. While it was easy for Cornelia to express her affection for the women around her in letters to her mother or in her diary entries and essays, it was difficult in person. Still, grateful for the afternoon's camaraderie, she came as close as she could to saying it out loud.

"What's so great about this for me," she said, "is that I'm meeting some of the most wonderful women!"

Fourteen

The WAFS quickly lost any illusion that they might blend in smoothly and quietly at New Castle. They were viewed alternately as guinea pigs, curios, and attractive young women by the thousands of men on the base, and they were still dogged by a steady throng of reporters from newspapers, magazines, and newsreels. Less than a month into their training, War Department publicist Hazel Taylor was trying to hold the press at bay. On October 2, she turned down interview requests from *The Philadelphia Inquirer* and others, saying that Nancy Love was "finding it most difficult to repair a pressing schedule already broken by conceding to publicity requests" and offering photos taken by a military photographer instead.

The scrutiny might well have disrupted such a program under ordinary circumstances, but, as Cornelia had come to realize, these were not ordinary women. "It speaks highly for the balance and common sense of these young women," said an ATC report, "that this public interest . . . seems not to have spoiled them or to have affected the quality of their work."

In reality, there was simply much more to worry about than a news-hungry press corps. Along with their course work and training, they had to deal with the vicissitudes of army life. They were, for instance, taught how to stand guard, although they would never do so. They were given firearms instruction, learning to tear down and rebuild .45s they were not permitted to fire. They were walked through a field containing samples of poisonous gases so they could learn to recognize them, then taken by two enlisted men into a small building and shown how to use gas masks. They stood for a moment, eyeing each other warily from behind their grasshopper-head masks, until one of the enlisted men set off a tear-gas canister. As was the case with male recruits, the WAFS were told to take off their masks and leave the building. Their eyes burning, they coughed and gasped and cried, to the hearty amusement of the enlisted men.

New WAFS continued to arrive. The phones rang constantly, and officers could frequently be found waiting in a front room of the BOQ to pick up WAFS for dates. Given the presence of Mrs. Anderson, the housekeeper, Nancy Batson said, "it was like being in a sorority in college."

The newer WAFS began their own round of training and spent little time with the original group, particularly as ferrying began. Still, they got some time to interact, and the first group tried to help the newcomers feel at home.

Nancy Batson recalled how Cornelia had walked down the hall to welcome her on her first day. "She was tall and slim and so friendly," said Batson, who was glad to hear another southern accent, "and you could tell she was well-bred and well-educated— just the perfect southern lady. She said, 'I'm Cornelia Fort. At five, I'll come and get you, and we'll go to the officers' club.' I didn't know anybody, and I'll never forget the way she took me under her wing."

By mid-October the WAFS were restlessly awaiting the orders that would take them on their first ferrying mission. As they wrapped up ground school and took their last flights, they socialized as they could and looked for ways to fill the time that stretched out before them.

Delaware's weather compounded the problem. On Tuesday, October 13, high winds kept the WAFS out of the air. Cornelia and Betty went in to New Castle for a cocktail party, leaving at seven to meet Nancy Love at the Hotel du Pont for what Betty called "a most enjoyable dinner accompanied by a swell bull session." Wednesday brought wind, rain, and fog that lasted essentially uninterrupted for four days. Their planes grounded, the WAFS spent the mornings in class on such subjects as first aid and military law and custom. In the afternoons they shopped or visited the beauty parlor. Cornelia had dinner on Wednesday and Friday nights at the home of Alice du Pont with some of the WAFS and a handful of senior officers from the base.

Cornelia had heard that the first few assignments might include a southern run, and on Wednesday, October 21, she sent a postcard home asking her mother if she would be willing to meet her at the airport, in the middle of night if necessary, and if she would bring Cornelia's dog, Kevin.

The anticipation was finally broken on Thursday, October 22, when Nancy Love learned the Piper assembly plant in Lock Haven had six Cubs ready for ferrying to Long Island's Mitchel Field. She gathered the first WAFS, whose ground and flight training was now completed, into a barracks meeting room and went over last-minute instructions. She warned them to stay 500 feet away from each other and used x's drawn on paper to show them the positions they should take as they flew. Cornelia, as navigator, would lead, with Pat, Helen Mary, Del, and Teresa flying in a loose V behind her. The flight leader, Betty, would trail until the very end, then land first.

There was an edge of unreality as they packed their big B-4 bags, which served as suitcases, took their parachute bags, and boarded a Boeing twin-engine transport for the flight to Lock Haven. For Cornelia, as for the other WAFS, the dream was coming true. All the hard work, all the patronizing, and all the extra hurdles the army had placed before them were paying off. They were finally going to ferry planes for the U.S. military. They looked out the windows of the big transport as best they could and tried to navigate for practice. The flight was uneventful until the end, when the pilot—a trainee on a practice run—made a terrible bouncing landing. The women shook their heads and laughed.

In Lock Haven, the women realized just how effective all those reporters and photographers had been. Hundreds of people had come out to see the WAFS, and as they entered the small Piper factory, they felt every eye in the place turn to them. "They would not have stared one half as much," said Teresa, "had we been freaks from the circus sideshow."

The WAFS feigned nonchalance as best they could, ignoring the stares and trying to pretend they were old hands at this sort of thing. They inspected the Cubs, signed for them, and gathered around a big table to pencil the flight plan onto their maps, pulling rulers and plastic navigational tools out of their cases and spreading them on the table. Their first stop, Betty decided, would be Allentown, Pennsylvania, near the New Jersey border.

"Somewhat self-consciously," Cornelia wrote, "we climbed into six L4-B's and took off across the Allegheny Mtns. . . . in a beautiful V-echelon formation."

With the aid of a 25-mph tailwind, they went east over the sparsely settled mountains and valleys of the region, with Cornelia in the lead and Betty in the rear. None of the planes had radios, and the women flew, Teresa recalled, "by the watch, the map, and our ground speed. We just marked a course on our maps every ten miles. You moved your finger along the map, and away you went." Cornelia's navigating style was to drift just a little toward the checkpoints on her map as she passed them. It was as if she were "mentally touching them for luck," Del said.

They crossed the Susquehanna River and came into Allentown after a smooth seventy-five-minute flight. While the Cubs were being refueled, the WAFS wrestled with the military forms they were filling out for the first time, and Betty decided there would not be time to make it to Mitchel Field by an hour before sundown. She called the Americus Hotel and booked rooms; they would stay the night in Allentown.

They tied down their planes, stowed their parachutes, and headed by taxi—a ride for which they knew they would not be reimbursed—to a Western Union office, where Betty wired the operations officer to let him know where they and—more important to the army—the planes were. Then they went to the hotel, their spirits soaring. Cornelia wrote her mother:

> All of us felt practically historic—the first female ferry pilots to have active duty. On arriving at the hotel we unanimously agreed that instead of having to "rough it" on trips, it was the height of luxury.
>
> Bathtubs instead of showers. Great soft beds instead of army cots, and a telephone to wake us instead of pounding on doors.

The next morning we left precisely at 8 and arrived at our destination, Mitchel Field, Long Island, where we heaved a thankful sigh that our first mission was completed without incident.

As was often her wont, Cornelia was not telling her mother the entire story. The second leg of the trip could easily have ended with one or more of the Cubs getting blown out of the sky. At the hotel, Betty had phoned her husband, Bud, who told her flying was halted along the New York waterfront because of aerial target practice by gunners at several defense positions in the area. Betty told the others she was wiring Mitchel Field base operations, "to let them know we're coming and to tell them to call off the guns for us."

The six took off in a light morning drizzle. As they reached the Atlantic, Betty took the lead, since she knew New York's air space so well, and the others moved into echelon position behind her, forming a long slanted line, like one half of a V. They flew over Coney Island, then over Brooklyn, circled a camouflaged Mitchel, and, after sixty-five minutes in the air, landed with six perfect touchdowns. Hauling their parachutes and flight bags, they walked into the terminal, where they were about to learn that the army was not always a smoothly oiled machine.

"We asked for these planes two months ago," the operations officer barked. "We don't need them now." Betty insisted that he had no choice but to sign the papers she handed him, and her steely determination held sway. As the WAFS prepared to leave, the telephone rang. It was Western Union, delivering the telegram Betty had sent a few hours earlier. The women were stunned. No one had been alerted to the fact that they were coming in, and they might well have been fired on, mistaken for target-towing planes. "If the guns had clobbered us," wrote Del, "we would have taken the future for women as pilots for the Army Air Force with us into the drink."

At the nearby Aviation Country Club, where Nancy, Betty, and Pat were members, the six changed, had a glass of sherry to celebrate, and sat down to lunch. Cornelia wrote:

> Being very hungry for good music I streaked into NY to Carnegie Hall to hear Bruno Walter conduct before meeting Mrs. McCain at "21" for a drink. All of us took the 6:30 train home. It's simply wonderful to be able to whip out our little book of travel tickets and know we will get space, by priority if necessary [WAFS could bump anyone but the president and his aides]. Actually it is fair because having flown all day we need sleep and rest on the way home for the next trip. Our uniforms, which are as yet devoid of insignia, created a great stir. People guessed everything from Air Raid Wardens to WAACs to Junior (Girl Scout) Commandos.

The WAFS returned by train with stories to tell and with the desire to do something about their uniforms, which they decided were hopelessly unflattering. The cut made the women look heavier than they were, and the trousers, even after alteration, hung abominably. Several of the women went back to Carlson's for more refinements.

The next day, they were again marching in review before Colonel Tunner. "With all 20 of us in uniform," Cornelia wrote her mother, "we presented quite a spectacle."

It rained all day Monday, and after a morning attending ground school, the WAFS got their first taste of something they would be doing a great deal of: waiting out foul weather in the Alert Room. There were a few sofas along its block walls, and tables and chairs where the women might kill time playing cards or, in Cornelia's case, reading while waiting for orders. On one wall a pegboard with a map and colored golf tees showed where the WAFS were at any given moment.

Cornelia was first to go out again, receiving the southern orders she had been expecting. When the weather cleared, she was to pick up an L4-B in Lock Haven and take it to Nashville's Berry Field, where she had learned to fly just two and a half years earlier. Cornelia sent a quick telegram to her mother, asking her to arrange a Friday night dinner with Garth and his family. WILL WIRE ARRIVAL TIME, she added. HOT DOG.

The weather remained bad, though, and Cornelia, as she would do often in the coming weeks when they were grounded, passed the time with cocktail parties at the officers' club, roller-skating excursions, and the movies. She wasn't always easy to please; she and Betty thought so little of the film *Desperate Journey,* starring Errol Flynn and Ronald Reagan as pilots shot down in Nazi-occupied Poland, that they left in the middle.

On Halloween, Cornelia finally made her run. Her mother and sister were waiting for her in Nashville, as were several local reporters and photographers. Her visit was front-page news in the Berry Field newsletter of the 4th Ferrying Group. She told the paper she and her fellow WAFS hoped "in a small way to help the war effort by releasing pilots for combat duty." After a twenty-four-hour stopover at Fortland, Cornelia caught a commercial airliner back to Wilmington.

Another weather-induced delay in new missions began to wear on the nerves of the WAFS. "I was welcomed back like a hero," Cornelia wrote to her mother a few days after her return, "and to my horror I found that none of the other girls had been on any trips—and still haven't. It's like a dry rot of morale which is deadly. And the far-reaching effects of such stagnation are too dreadful to contemplate."

Such concerns, of course, never reached the press, which was still enthralled with the WAFS. Requests for interviews and photographs continued to pour in, and the ATC came to realize that more than just valuable time was at stake. "A public relations problem existed from the outset," the ATC noted. "It was inherent in the fact that these pilots were women, that they were generally young and not unattractive. The danger of over-glamorization, excessive sentimentality, and also of scandal was ever-present."

By the end of October, Colonel Tunner threw up his hands. The women under his command were on front pages all over the country, reporters were everywhere, there was always the fear that someone might turn up in flagrante delicto, and they had thus far moved exactly seven planes from point A to point B. Tunner fired off a missive to the War Department's Bureau of Public Relations, saying, "Because the disproportionate publicity which the W.A.F.S. has received seems inconsistent with the nature, scope and accomplishment of this squadron; and because this publicity has actually been interfering with the operations of the squadron; the Ferrying Division of the Air Transport Command believes that it will be advisable to cease all widespread publicity on the W.A.F.S. until definite and substantial results of the experiment may be observed."

The military encouraged the women to spend some of their downtime in the Link Trainers, the flight simulators some of the WAFS referred to as "Maytag Messerschmitts." "I have had four hours ($60 worth) in two days and am much happier about my enforced idleness," Cornelia wrote her mother, adding,

> When I actually noticed some improvement in my Link work today I simply beamed with happiness. And I guess that's as good an answer as any to your question of whether I felt I had to do this work. It's something so deep inside of me—a need so vital to my happiness as sunshine and sleep—I want more than I ever wanted anything in my life to be really good, to be a scientific pilot and command respect from all comers in aviation but even more important, for my own satisfaction and so, my dear, I guess that's it.

On Saturday, November 7, ATC commander General George came to New Castle to review the base parade and its contingent of WAFS. "Seems wicked for generals to stop the war for a bit of ritual," Cornelia wrote her mother, "but apparently that's the kind of war it is." For half an hour, as flags waved and bands played, thousands of men marched in squadrons past the general and a contingent of other officers on the reviewing stand. Finally it was the turn of the two little columns of WAFS to march smartly by. Nancy brought them to a halt and barked a "Left face!" command that turned them toward the assembled brass. The entire group of officers left the stand and walked toward the WAFS, who realized they were about to be given microscopic attention. The women knew at once that their columns had been too close together; as they made their left turn, the back row was nearly on top of the front row. They were afraid to move, though, so there they stood.

The officers walked from one end of the front row to the other, looking the WAFS up and down and chatting with each. When they got to the end of the line, the women sighed with relief, figuring that was it. Instead, the brass decided to inspect the second row also. That meant the officers had to work their way through an awkward gauntlet, walking sideways and conducting face-to-face chats with a row of women who were sucking in their chins, stomachs, and chests, sometimes to no avail, and trying desperately not to laugh.

Cornelia described the visit to her mother:

> I would not blame the rest of the men on the field for being fed up with the *entirely* unsolicited & unwelcome attention given the WAFS. [General George] merely walked down the front of the men's squadrons but he inspected us each & every one & stopped to chat with each of us. And to make us even more conspicuous, five WAFS were invited to have luncheon with him & his aides in the mess. The only table with a tablecloth, flowers, etc., and we sat thru the entire meal with a barrage of stares from everyone else in the mess. I had already eaten my lunch & was getting up to leave when Col. Baker came for me & told me I was supposed to have lunch at the Gen's. table. As I sat directly on his left I couldn't skip course after course so I manfully chewed my way thru another meal. He's a nice little man.

After two more days of killing time, Cornelia again wrote her mother:

11/9/42

Mother dear—

Note the date—a full week since I left you & I still
haven't gone out—except for the Link Trainers it has been a
totally useless week. I'm leading a flight of two—giving the
other girl experience—to Selma, Ala, which will take me
thru Atlanta and probably airline thru Nashville.

It has been a pleasant week socially. Mrs. Walter
Carpenter (he is the Pres. of Du Pont Co.) gave a small
dinner party for me. The roast turkey & cranberry sauce we
had there shall in all likelihood be my Thanksgiving.

I met a slap-happy pilot at the Officers' Club after the
movie one night & he took me dinner-dancing the next
night. I hadn't realized how hungry for dancing I was. So
very few of the officers here are worth walking across the
street to chat with. I've never seen such a group of charmless
men. Collectively their attractiveness is very low. Jimmy is
fun & funny so it was pleasant.

Bud Gillies (Betty's delightful husband) flew a twin-
engined Grumman down on Sat. and they took Nancy & me
to dinner at our favorite, the Brandywine Room. To sit
down with 3 people who are so utterly like people we have
known & to be happily at ease is a rarity here instead of
commonplace. You wouldn't believe there could be such a
large percentage of strikingly commonplace men as we have
collected. . . .

Yesterday was gray & rainy so we spent the afternoon in
front of the fire at the Club reading. I met a guy (one of the
best pilots on the field) who promises to add a little interest.

He's going to try to arrange a trip in a Bomber (B-26) with
me as his Co-Pilot. As Gen. George told me flatly that if we
did well (& he was tremendously impressed that I had taken a
plane to Nashville by myself) in a few months we would be
allowed to fly anything we were capable of. This Bill
Howard is from West Virginia & a very attractive person,
the first one I've seen.

Cornelia's trip to Selma was part of November 9 orders that
ended the long flying drought for the early WAFS. Cornelia, Betty,
Barbara Poole, B.J. Erickson, Barbara Towne, Teresa James, and
Helen Richards, along with three lieutenants, were ordered to
the Piper factory. Betty and Teresa would take planes to Lake
Charles, Louisiana; the two Barbaras to Jackson, Mississippi;
Cornelia and Helen to Selma; and B.J. Erickson to New Orleans.
There was a mad dash to pack and pick up orders before catch-
ing the train to Philadelphia, where the group had dinner, took
in the movie *Wake Island,* and then boarded the 1:03 A.M. train
for Lock Haven.

Teresa had a habit of cutting up during train and plane rides,
especially when there were male pilots along. Spirits were always
high on such trips, and while Betty felt the need to keep a loose
lid on things—to project at least an image of seriousness—Teresa
took it as her mission to lighten things up. She looked down at
her hands and began, very dramatically and seriously, to "sew."
The garment was imaginary, but her demeanor was such that the
lieutenants were caught completely unprepared. They studied her,
unsure what to think. They squinted, looked at one another, and
looked back at her. Cornelia and the other WAFS were virtually

on the floor by the time the guys figured out they were being taken for a ride.

"A merry crew," wrote Betty in her diary that night. "Quite a time getting tucked away in Pullman berths."

They pulled into Lock Haven at 6:40 A.M., "weary and bedraggled," and spent the day at the Fallon Hotel, hoping the weather would clear. It didn't.

The next day, at 11:45 A.M., they left Lock Haven in their L4-Bs and made their first fuel stop in Middletown, Pennsylvania. Minus one of the lieutenants, they flew in formation to Virginia's Quantico marine base, where they found the kind of warm welcome they didn't always get from military men.

Cornelia later wrote:

> Quantico, that Marine haven of masculinity, is one of our most favorite! We invaded their airport for gas one day to the utter astonishment of the enlisted men on duty, who said in voices shaken with bits of shattered historical precedent, "You-all are the first lady pilots ever to land on this airport."

The WAFS planned flights day to day, with weather and mileage dictating each leg's destination, and they quickly learned they could take nothing for granted. At their next stop, in Charlottesville, Virginia, Cornelia and another of the WAFS came in on a grassy field that had seen more than its share of rain in recent weeks. Both found their wheels sinking into the muddy runway as they landed, and momentum threw both planes onto their noses, breaking the propellers. Luckily, neither pilot was hurt, and the rest of the crew searched for dryer parts of the field and landed safely.

Although they had received no warning about the mud and there had been no way to tell the condition of the field from the air, the WAFS were embarrassed about the incident. Cornelia and the second pilot had to wait in Charlottesville for new props for their planes, while the others headed toward Spartanburg, South Carolina.

Cornelia stayed with friends in Charlottesville and in Lynchburg, before flying to Atlanta for a reunion with brothers Dudley and Rufus. As she wrote her mother, she even managed to work in a visit with Clen Robertson.

I phoned Clen to say hello & he said he could come up which was a total surprise. I slept from 11–2 & he came about 2:30 so we had a few sleepy hours together. He is very thin & looks older but very fit.

I delivered my plane at 2:30, jumped into a plane that was warming up for me, & roared 50 miles to catch an airliner. Douglas "Wrong Way" Corrigan, who is also in the Ferry Command, rode partway with me. He's a very nice, twinkly-eyed little guy.

With my priority I put a col. off the plane. He was a little irked but more gracious than I'd have been. I slept all the way back, waking up only to eat, read *Life* & *Time*, & collapse again.

When she arrived back at New Castle, Cornelia found a wire from Bill McCain. He had been transferred from the *Indianapolis* and had returned to New York by way of San Francisco. Cornelia wrote her mother:

I called him in NY & he came right down. It's too damn bad I can't have leave while he does but it's out of the question. I was fairly sure I wouldn't be sent out the same day but I was almost wrong.

He arrived at 5:30 & we went out to the officers' club so he could meet Nancy and Betty. He has been in Alaska for 5 months, which is apparently deadly.

We went into the Brandywine Room & had lobster thermidor & champagne for celebration. It was wonderful to see him again but oh damn how hard for me.

He has 10 days leave & a 6 wks course in Washington. He begged me to marry him now so we could have 6 wks together & that I would belong to him when he went back to sea. I wanted to say yes but Mother dear, I simply can't. I love him tenderly & devotedly, our interests are identical, we have an incredible lot in common but my heart doesn't pound even the slightest bit, I have nothing that resembles passion for him & so my heart & my mind made me say no. He was so stricken it made me weep.

He had said that all he wanted to talk to his family about was how wonderful he thought I was but instead all they talked about was how wonderful they thought I was. His mother told him as he left that she hoped he would come back with my yes & that she could have me as a daughter. So possibly you can guess how hard it was for me.

If I can work Xmas leave he is coming to Nashville with me. He is crazy to meet you.

Today he came out at 11, brought me roses, & took me out to breakfast. No sooner had I reported back to the base than I found orders waiting for me. So even the chance of seeing him in Wilmington is shot to hell. Five of us left at 2:30 by plane & here we are again [at the Hotel Fallon in Lock Haven]. This hotel is getting as familiar as Fortland.

I'm going south again & confidentially I can tell you that I will eat dinner at Antoine's—I'll go thru Atlanta again & hope I can work it for overnight. I'm in a state of near collapse again so my darling I will say good night and send you all my

Love,
Cornelia

The orders, for Cornelia, Betty, Teresa, B.J. Erickson, and Barbara Towne had come on November 17, after a day spent filling out paperwork, including a report for Group Operations on the nose-up landings in Charlottesville. "Mad dash to repack, collect maps, and get ready to take off at 2:30 in the Lodestar for Lock Haven," wrote Betty.

The WAFS were expected to be ready at a moment's notice, so packing was generally a hurried affair. Then again, there wasn't much to take. Maps and paperwork went into a leather briefcase. The rest they threw into small canvas sports bags, which they often carried instead of their big B-4 bags. In would go underwear, socks, a toothbrush, high heels, and perhaps some leg makeup, something many women wore in place of stockings, which were hard to come by, as well as the skirt and blouse each was required to wear on the return trip. The women learned quickly to wash out their shirts and underwear in hotel sinks and to dry shirts on hotel radiators. Cornelia would later write:

Like most people in the services, laundry is our major problem—specifically shirts. Certainly no laundry today will provide overnite service and even when you are weatherbound for several days in a town you don't dare turn loose a shirt, for as soon as it is gone the sun will begin to shine and off you will fly, leaving your lonely shirt. Some of us have shirts scattered across ten states. But finally you come to the method used by most of us of washing the shirt one nite and having another hotel in the next town iron it.

On Wednesday, November 18, despite relatively poor weather, the group flew to Middletown, Pennsylvania, to refuel, and then to Quantico to spend the night. Cornelia dropped a postcard to her mother.

These Marines are fabulous. They never blinked an eye when 5 females asked for quarters. They simply blocked off a corridor and tacked up a LADIES sign—took us to the officers' club for champagne. What a good group of guys!

She sent Bill a similar if somewhat toned-down card. The visit had quickly turned into quite an adventure. After the officers' club, where Teresa remembered most of them drinking old-fashioneds, a large group went out for dinner and then came back for more drinks at the club. For Cornelia, it was a grown-up version of a party at West Point or Yale.

The blocked-off second-floor corridor was in the Transient Officers' Quarters, and the officers in question were to make arrangements to spend the night elsewhere. The job had been done so quickly, though, that one officer didn't get the word. He came back to the BOQ, apparently in an advanced state of inebriation, and was unable to find his room. He found the one Teresa had been given, undressed, and promptly passed out. Teresa came in late to find him out cold, in his underwear, on her bed.

Wanting only to sleep, she found a corporal and asked him if he wouldn't get the marine out of her bed. He went into her room and came back out, wide-eyed.

"Ma'am," he said, "that's a major. There's nothing I can do about him."

"Well, will you at least get my clothes out of there and get me another room?" she asked.

As she and the corporal headed for her new room, Cornelia, who had had quite enough to drink herself, was wandering around the corridor looking for soap. At about 2 A.M., Teresa settled in. She woke at six when her door rattled and swung open. Cornelia came in from the hallway, naked except for the towel she held against her, as drunk, Teresa thought, as she'd ever seen anyone. Cornelia had apparently passed out while taking a bath or shower somewhere down the hall before waking and finding her way to Teresa's room. As Teresa watched, Cornelia crossed the room, went into the bathroom, crawled into the tub, as she had done so often in the Manhattan hotels she shared with her Sarah Lawrence friends, and fell asleep.

The WAFS rose a short time later, and a groggy Cornelia paid the price for her indulgence. She walked blearily into the mess to be confronted with her bête noíre, a huge platter of steaming sunny-side-up eggs. She turned with what little grace she could muster under the circumstances and ran out the door.

Haze kept the WAFS grounded until 10 A.M., when they were finally able to get airborne. They headed toward Richmond, with Cornelia hungover and operating on little sleep, and stopped for fuel. After another fueling stop at Lynchburg, they went on to Winston-Salem, where Teresa and Barbara Poole's mission was completed, and where the others had a leisurely dinner at the Robert E. Lee Hotel and remained overnight.

On the twentieth, one-mile visibility kept Betty, Cornelia, and Barbara Towne grounded all morning, but at 1 P.M. they were able to leave for Charlotte and then go on to Greenville. Betty's mission was completed there, and she caught a commercial flight back to Washington and the base. Barbara and Cornelia, who was finally feeling a little better, continued toward their final destination of Biloxi, Mississippi.

On Thanksgiving Day, Cornelia again wrote to her mother.

A very happy Thanksgiving and golly how I wish I were with you. I'm going to have Thanksgiving dinner with Bill either at Mrs. Dick du Pont's or in Baltimore, depending on my orders. This is a working day for us.

My trip was very satisfactory. The first night at Quantico was very colorful indeed. The Marines outdid themselves in hospitality, the 2nd night in Winston-Salem where I had a very fine steak with an old friend, the 3rd night in Spartanburg, S.C., which was dreary, the 4th night with Rufus & Ag, which was as good as an unexpected Xmas present. Dud & Pearl met us at the Piedmont Driving Club. It was so gay to go out at 10 instead of going to bed at 10. How delightful it was to dance again.

You've no idea the vast benefits that fall to me now that I'm in the Army. We were weather bound at Maxwell all morning & a Lt. asked me if I'd like an hour's twin-engine time. In civilian life I could have begged & pleaded & offered $100 & still wouldn't have gotten it. I said "yes of course," so now I have an hour of twin motored time all legal & everything. I was speechless with excitement. The next nite I spent in Mobile with Ann Perdue's family. I had an elegant dinner in that most beautiful old house, we talked long distance to Ann, who is to have a baby in Jan, & I had breakfast in bed! Oh my! I delivered my ship to Biloxi (a military secret altho these airplanes have so little military value we can tell their destination). The Gulf was lovely & blue.

We were flown to New Orleans—80 miles along the lovely coast line, beaches & palm trees etc. Lunch at Arnaud's & a ramble thru the French Quarter. I succumbed to the lure of Antique shops & bought a soup tureen for the Andrews. It is a beautiful—very plain—one & I hope you'll approve of it.

Dinner at Antoine's was quite a ritual. Oysters Rockefeller, pompano in a paper bag, a bottle of white Bordeaux & crêpes suzettes—during which they dim the lights so you can better appreciate the beauty of the flame. Some soldier at the next table—after the lights had been dimmed several times—remarked in a loud voice, "What the hell is wrong with these lights?" which amused us & horrified the waiter.

We saw or heard the last half of the New Orleans Symphony concert, took the midnite plane, & got home yesterday. Bill came up from Washington last nite because we were afraid I might be sent out today. We had lobster & sauterne & it was very good to see him. I'm enclosing his last letter—please save it.

Despite Cornelia's tearful refusal of his marriage proposal, Bill's letter made clear that his ardor had not cooled.

Darling,

Being with you that brief while in Delaware was a brief vision of heaven, an all too short glimpse of that sun which has been hidden so long from me by the exigencies of war. . . .

When we parted in Honolulu, so many ages ago, I thought that I loved you very much. [But now a] passion so much stronger, so much more overwhelming has seized me that I can't even think straight. Day and night I dream of one thing, see one name before me. . . . You were so right when you said that we should wait, and know each other better, and not rush blindly into anything, because by doing so you have bound me to you so strongly that nothing can ever untie us. Seeing you again under different conditions simply makes me love you a thousand times more strongly. It was terribly hard to have to tear myself away before you took off. . . .

I received your postcard [sent the first night of her Quantico visit] today, and was happy to learn that you had

gotten well started on your flight and were in good hands.
The Marines are wonderful people and, as you pointed out
so charmingly, are equal to any situation. Honey, I am
praying for you and hoping that you will not run into any
more quagmires.

All my love,

Bill

Fifteen

As sparse as their flying time had been, the WAFS continued to draw press attention. Colonel Tunner and War Department publicist Hazel Taylor had slowed the initial media barrage somewhat, but it had by no means stopped. Nancy Love had long since grown weary of the interruptions, and the pressure was beginning to show. She was fielding requests for speaking engagements, radio shows, and press interviews for herself and the other WAFS while recruiting and interviewing new flyers and scheduling her growing contingent. One afternoon, Nancy found herself juggling rescheduling requests for a *Life* magazine photographer, a *Harper's Bazaar* editor, and a *Baltimore Sun* reporter just as Taylor stopped for a visit. Nancy, who was out of patience, told Taylor she just wanted to have such interruptions "over and done with." Then, as Taylor prepared for her next visit, Nancy told her not to come, stating both that Taylor had given her no good reason for the stop and that her most photogenic pilots were all on missions.

In a scathing November 20 report, Taylor wrote:

> It is my professional opinion that the best public relations with the press could not result from Mrs. Love's meeting with writers, editors, or photographers in her present state of mind. . . . Were I a psychologist I might explain the situation in terms of "thresholds" or "psychology of fatigue" and all that. Were it within my province, I would advise the Ferrying Division of

the Air Transport to send her on a few weeks of ferrying planes to give her the fun of flying, and bring a deputy administrator pilot in to relieve her for a time of constant administrative work. Were I without faith in humankind, loyalty to womankind, and not possessed of a government job, I could write you an inspired essay entitled SPOILED BRAT.

Nancy wanted desperately to get in the air again, and she got her wish on November 26, when she joined Cornelia in delivering a pair of Cubs to Camp Edwards, Massachusetts. As she and Cornelia landed their tiny planes on the base's small, windy airfield, Nancy was reminded dramatically of the difficulty of the WAFS' missions. Nancy landed first in a strong crosswind, with Cornelia right behind her. They taxied to the parking area in front of the hangar, and Cornelia cut her engine off. Nancy, mindful of the havoc a strong wind can wreak with a tiny plane, kept hers running so she could control it until help came.

Cornelia realized her own mistake almost instantly. The Cub began to turn at the mercy of the wind, its wings wobbling. Cornelia jumped out and grabbed the strut but was unable to hang on. The plane began to spin. Its wing passed over her, and before she knew it she was struck on the head by the propeller and knocked to her knees.

There was nothing Nancy could do without abandoning her own Cub, and she sat watching, using her aileron and brakes to maintain the plane's position. Finally, a man came running from behind the hangar to help Cornelia push the plane to a better spot. Once it was there, Cornelia hung on gamely as the man walked to Nancy's plane. Only after he had signed for it would Nancy cut the engine and climb out.

The WAFS had entered a period of intense activity. There were often lines at the phones in BOQ 14 as women who had planned dates for the evening waited to call and break them after getting orders. Flying in tiny planes, without radios, in the face of highly changeable weather was difficult and often exhausting, and Cornelia was put off by attempts to glamorize it. Still, despite continued skepticism and ridicule from male pilots, she remained as thrilled by her work as by anything she had ever done. She was equally glad that the WAFS' pioneering work helped open the door for a training school in Sweetwater, Texas. There, Jackie Cochran, who had returned from England, was training women pilots who would be called the Women's Airforce Service Pilots, or WASPs. Cornelia would write:

> That there were men with their tongues in their cheeks goes without saying, men waiting for us to get lost or crack up or prove in some way the undependability of women pilots. Our probationary period is up, our contracts extended, and there are girls in Texas being trained to join us. So far we have done a good job and I say this thankfully and with all possible fingers crossed. We have delivered airplanes, numbers of airplanes, without getting lost and without cracking up.
>
> We have no hopes of replacing men pilots. Numerically we are too small to have ever conceived of such an idea. But we can each release a man to combat, to faster ships, to overseas work. Naturally we hope to have a chance to fly bigger planes. All pilots do. But the planes we fly, regardless of their size or

speed, have to be delivered. Delivering a trainer to Texas may be as important as delivering a bomber to Africa if you take the long view. We want to prove and we are beginning to prove that women can be trusted to deliver airplanes safely and in the doing serve the country which is our country too.

I have yet to have a feeling which approaches in satisfaction that of having signed, sealed, and delivered an airplane for the United States Army. The attitude that most nonflyers have about pilots is distressing and often acutely embarrassing. They chatter about the glamour of flying. Well, any pilot can tell you how glamorous it is. We get up in the cold dark in order to get to the airport by dawn. If the weather is good we fly all day, usually without lunch. We wear heavy cumbersome flying suits and 30-pound parachutes. We are either cold or hot and you can't change clothes very well in the air. We get sunburns and windburns and if female your lipstick wears off and your hair gets straighter and straighter. You look forward all afternoon to the bath you will have and the steak. Well, we get the bath but sometimes we are too tired to eat the steak and we fall wearily into bed.

None of us can put into words why we fly. It is something different for each of us. I can't *say* exactly why I fly but I *know* why as I've never known anything in my life. . . . I know it in dignity and self-sufficiency and the pride of skill. I know it in the satisfaction of usefulness.

As rough as the flying could be, there was nothing worse for the WAFS than inactivity, usually caused by the weather. Early in December, Betty and B.J. Erickson were in Albany, Georgia, grounded by rain that fell through the first night and kept falling for a second and then a third day. The leader of a mission had to wire the base each night with a status report. Betty would wire THREE, the coded message that told the base they were weathered in. She would send her husband the same message at the Grumman factory.

By the third day, the two of them were bored to death. The weather had been routinely awful in Delaware most of the fall, and it was bad here. They had done their Christmas shopping, had their uniforms altered yet again, and found a dozen other ways to kill time. Still, there was no end in sight.

That evening, Betty sent her husband a telegram that said simply HEBREWS 13:8. Bud and those around him had never seen a message like it. The telephone operator at Grumman called Western Union back to make sure she had gotten it right. Eventually, someone in the factory said, "It sounds like she's referring to the Bible."

There was not a Bible to be found at the plant, so men began calling their wives. Finally, a voice came over the phone, reading from a family Bible: "Hebrews 13:8: 'Jesus Christ the same yesterday, and to day, and for ever.'"

The weather was bad throughout the East, and Cornelia took advantage of the downtime to write her mother on December 8 from the Sanborn Hotel in Florence, South Carolina, where she and Barbara Towne were staying during an L4-B delivery to Carrabelle, Florida.

Mother dear—

This far & no farther have we gotten. I wonder if the time will ever come when I can get up and not care how

bad the weather is. It has surely fouled us up on the
trip.

We were weather bound 3½ days in Lock Haven, a
town with very few facilities for fun. . . . The next nite
we were 50 miles farther south in the dreary little town
of Lumberton, N.C. The only entertainment possible for
2 girls in a strange town is the movies & even the movies
were closed there.

I'm so dreadfully tired of bad restaurants. I should have
learned by now that I will never get a good meal in a small-
town café but somehow hunger makes me forget & I'm
disappointed anew every meal.

I miss you very much & I thought of you constantly all
day Sunday, the anniversary of Pearl Harbor. Certainly last
year I had no inkling or foreknowledge that I would be in
Lumberton, N.C., a town I'd never heard of, doing a job
which was still unheard of. The war has brought us many
changes, the main one in my case being a heightened
enjoyment of the very simplest things—a candle-lit dinner &
a drink with friends before a fire—things I took utterly for
granted in my prewar life which seems several lifetimes ago.

Aloha nui—

Cornelia

Dead towns and bad restaurants were by no means their only
hardships. WAFS flew tiny planes, often with open cockpits, in frigid
weather and in windy conditions, using maps they would hold
open on their laps. (At first, several flyers had maps fly out of their
hands and flutter uselessly away until they learned simply to strap

them to their legs.) Their feet would go numb. The wind would slow them down dramatically. There were frequent fuel stops, particularly in the face of headwinds, and a civilian field might have only car gasoline, which had to be strained through a chamois cloth. And of course the WAFS, like male pilots, sometimes got lost or made forced landings. There was no certainty about where a pilot might spend the night.

Cornelia wrote about one such episode on a southeastern trip:

In leading a flight of observation planes thru Georgia, we were forced to land on a highway. Funny now but I remember how dry my mouth was at the time. Those planes are designed for short reconnaissance flights and haven't sufficient gasoline for long trips or for unfavorable weather.

Either the wind information given me was incorrect or it increased mightily, for after ¾ of the journey I realized it would be very close. We came down to the treetops in order to avoid as much headwind as possible, but as we inched forward it became apparent that even that wouldn't get us there. The fields were ridged and small and heartbreakingly full of stumps. After the gas gauge sat on empty for 10 min. I decided I had better choose a place to land before it was chosen for me. A lovely beautiful wonderful highway came rolling into view and it took me hardly a moment to realize just how particularly wonderful a highway it was. It ran into the wind and was totally without telephone wires but best of all it was long and flat and provided a view of traffic, something there was fortunately none of.

I landed gingerly and looked back with tremendous relief to see the other plane land beautifully and so up the road we taxied to a place we could pull off and park our air chariots. We were so delighted to have the planes safely down we forgot to realize how ridiculous we looked. A truck almost went into the ditch at the sight of us prancing up the highway.

When I asked the filling station operator what octane his gas was he chewed reflectively on his cigar and finally said rightly, "Octane! I don't know, lady. All I know is that it's mighty cheap car gas." And it was. But it took us sputtering safely into our destination. I was so afraid that even with my gov. forms he would demand gas-ration coupons that I hardly gave any thought to the octane count.

As Cornelia had noted, the Piper Cub, for all its assets both as a small one-person plane and for military reconnaissance, was not designed for comfortable long flights.

"They were hard to fly across country," Betty said. "You were cold in the wintertime and you had no radio. The hardest work we did was ferrying Cubs. It was much easier when you got a bigger aircraft that was more stable, was able to take care of the weather better, and had better instruments."

Given a stiff headwind, a Cub, which was rated at 70 mph, could slow to the point where cars on the highways below would pass it. As winter came—and it can come early in the mountains of Pennsylvania, where they picked the Cubs up—navigation became a nightmare. "It all looked the same," said Betty. "What you usually use in spring, summer, and fall are the streams and the rivers, and they were all frozen over. They were all white with snow on top of the ice. You could get so lost in that territory. If you got off course a little bit, you couldn't find anything you recognized."

During winter the flying uniform changed as well. There were the lambskin-lined two-piece monkey suits, so bulky that mechanics would usually have to help the women put on their parachutes and squeeze into the planes, as well as gloves, boots, helmets, and goggles. In the Cubs, which had cabins, that would be enough, but in the Fairchilds, which had open cockpits, it was a different story. Then, Teresa said, "The clothing wasn't warm—just heavy." There were also chamois face masks that left the mouth and nose exposed and reminded the WAFS of actor Lon Chaney, known for horror films like *The Phantom of the Opera*. It was often not enough. The below-freezing air could be blowing by at 70 miles an hour throughout a flight. The WAFS would gulp coffee at refueling stops and try to warm themselves. There were times their fingers were too numb to tackle the zippers on their flying suits.

Then there was the fact that, should the need arise, the women had no means to empty their bladders of all that coffee. The men used relief tubes, black funnel-like pieces of rubber they pulled from under the seat and urinated into. With an extraordinary degree of stripping, agility, and concentration, a woman could learn to use one, but with extremely rare warm-weather exceptions, the women learned simply to avoid drinking much before a flight.

All this became fodder for conversation among the women in the BOQ. They would also discuss the fact that, since so many had been instructors, they often ran into men they had taught to fly, men who now flew bigger planes than they had ever been permitted to fly. They discussed the improvised logistics, the late-night arrivals, the difficulty finding places to eat, and the many short nights before waking, bone-weary, in the dark for another long day of flying. They were constantly amazed at public reaction to their uniforms. Many people were unable to believe these women flew military airplanes. They were taken for airline stewardesses, members of the Mexican Army, Red Cross volunteers, ferryboat pilots, and even motorcyclists. Being out of uniform didn't always help. On occasion, when they would check into a hotel as a group, people thought they were prostitutes.

Cornelia remembered a taxi driver in Winston-Salem who, "upon recognizing the standard GI suitcases issued to us in the Ferry Command, asked the bellboy how many ferry pilots there were and was told indignantly, 'They ain't no ferry pilots; them's soldier women.'"

Then there was her "unbelievable" experience "in the sacred and expensive precincts of Antoine's ladies' room in New Orleans. An elderly lady asked us what our uniforms represented. Having learned that WAFS is an unfamiliar term to most, I answered as simply and concisely as possible that we were ferry pilots. She nodded brightly and turned to her friend. 'That's why I didn't know. We don't have a ferry in our town.'"

But none of it—not even the most difficult days they faced—took the luster off the job. Evelyn Sharp wrote to an aunt and uncle, "I meet so many interesting people. I can't think of a better job. I have shelter, food, clothing, money in the bank, get to travel and meet people, have good times, and do the job I want to do and at the same time serve my country. No, sir, they don't make better jobs."

Cornelia continued to run into friends. During one southeast run, she stopped overnight in south-central Georgia, calling her old flight instructor, Aubrey Blackburne, and asking him to meet her. Cornelia's interests and her relationship with Aubrey had not changed. "We spent the whole time discussing low-frequency range stations and instrument flying," he said. "As it worked out, that was the last time I ever saw the child."

In early December, the squadron reached its planned total of 25 members with the arrivals of Bernice Batten and Dorothy Scott, who finished their course work and began ferrying on the twenty-first. The squadron also reached an important milestone: It had become, in the eyes of the Army Air Corps, a viable and valuable part of the war effort. The WAFS' delivery record was as good as or better than that of the men, and they handled everything from weather to paperwork admirably in the face of an often rugged schedule. In fact, when Teresa James led a 23-plane flight from Montana to Tennessee, the first 6 planes to land were piloted by the only 6 women on the flight, all WAFS. Two days later, only 6 of the 17 men had arrived. The other 11 had gotten lost or had stopped for unauthorized visits along the way.

The WAFS' early successes had come at an opportune time. No one denied the need for pilots. The number of male flyers had increased sevenfold during 1942, from fewer than 400 to 2,800, but the need remained great. Now the ATC was hatching a plan to form WAFS units at other bases near plane manufacturers—which would provide more than a thousand women with the opportunity to fly for the military. The original 25 women would be split into smaller groups to guide the new units, to be located at Dallas; Long Beach, California; and Romulus, Michigan, and filled with graduates of Jackie Cochran's new training school in Sweetwater.

The WAFS' success also meant that many of the early flight restrictions on them had been lifted or were being ignored. They could now fly on missions with men, and there were plans to allow them to fly faster, more powerful planes after their transfers to the new bases. Those planes appealed greatly to Nancy Love, who by now had had more than enough of desk work and an occasional flight in a tiny training plane. She had been visiting the new sites, and within days she would request and receive a transfer to Dallas.

Despite the expansion of their role, the WAFS would not, as they hoped, become part of the military, with the added benefits that status would bring. On Saturday, December 12, the ninety-day civilian appointments of Cornelia and the rest of the original WAFS were extended. The exception was Aline Rhonie, who had complained once too often about the way the WAFS and the base were run, and who had delayed her return to the base after one trip so she could visit her family.

The following Monday, five WAFS—Cornelia, Betty, Helen Richards, Evelyn Sharp, and Dorothy Fulton, a new member with 2,500 hours of flying time—and six civilian male flyers headed by train to Lock Haven, arriving Tuesday morning.

It had been bitterly cold, and it snowed throughout the day. The group sat idle all morning, and then Cornelia and Betty took in an afternoon movie, watching *Now, Voyager* with Bette Davis and Paul Henreid, a film they enjoyed immensely. They followed that with a Swedish massage.

When the weather finally cleared, they undertook their ferrying runs. Betty flew to Syracuse, New York; Helen and Evelyn to Indiana; and Cornelia and Dorothy to Dyersburg, Tennessee. Then all of them made their way back to a frigid New Castle.

As Christmas approached, each of the WAFS tried to line up holiday leave. Cornelia had been asked by the McCains to spend Christmas in New York, but she sent gifts and told them she would spend her short leave visiting her mother. She had changed a great deal in the past two years, but Fortland and family were still her emotional anchors. Time was too precious and Cornelia's life too unpredictable for her to pass up the chance to go home.

Mrs. Fort had temporarily moved to her son Rufus's house in the Belle Meade section of Nashville early in December; Fortland was simply too much to keep up and help was impossible to find during the war. Still, Cornelia drove out to the empty mansion during her stay, depositing her carefully kept diaries, which contained a detailed history of her months with the WAFS. There they joined the other diaries she had kept since childhood. Cornelia had long been concerned for their safety, and she knew they would be secure in the tiny bedroom that still boasted the over-the-door propeller she had installed there during her first days as a pilot.

Her old friend Elizabeth Craig planned a luncheon for Cornelia during her visit and invited a group of her friends, many of whom she had not seen since before Pearl Harbor. On Christmas Day, though, a major storm hit the city, dumping three inches of sleet, snapping trees, and making travel hazardous. The storm would last three days.

"I'd gone all-out trying to have the most wonderful meal," Elizabeth recalled. "I remember I had fresh crabmeat and fresh raspberries and all these things, and all of Cornelia's oldest and dearest friends were coming to lunch to see her because none of us had seen her since the situation in Honolulu. Nobody got there. And then the trees started crashing through the roof."

Cornelia's flight back to Wilmington took her through Washington, D.C., and from there she dropped her mother an American Airlines postcard. "There aren't any words to tell you how much I love you & how the memory of Christmas will be with me always & forever. Cornelia."

That sweet memory was to be short-lived. On the twenty-seventh, after a session in the Link Trainer and a drink at the officers' club, Cornelia received yet another life-changing telegram, this one from Clen Robertson in Nashville:

FIRE FROM DEFECTIVE WIRING BURNED FORTLAND COM-
PLETELY THIS MORNING ABOUT TEN NO ONE HURT YOUR
MOTHER IS WELL CONSIDERING THE SHOCK GARTH AND RUFUS
NOTIFIED MOST OF THE THINGS DOWNSTAIRS WERE SAVED BUT
NOTHING UPSTAIRS ALL MY LOVE AND SYMPATHY LET
ME KNOW OF ANY FURTHER INFORMATION YOU WANT OR
ANYTHING I CAN DO. CLEN.

Epperson had discovered the fire and called both the fire department and Mrs. Fort. Firefighters had the blaze under control in an hour, but then they exhausted the 10,000-gallon cistern in the yard and the fire spread again. Firemen, policemen, and the remaining servants and farm workers were able to save many of the first-floor furnishings, but nothing on the second floor. Well over $100,000 in paintings, furnishings, books, carpets, clothing, jewelry, and pianos was destroyed. Much of the front page of Monday morning's *Tennessean* was devoted to the story, which noted that the second fire engine on the scene had been christened the Rufus E. Fort after the doctor died, less than three years earlier.

In a few hours, Cornelia had lost virtually every material possession. Her clothes, books, photographs, letters, childhood keepsakes, and diaries were all destroyed. She let the news sink in for a moment, then wandered down the hall to Del's room.

"She was so stupefied that it was difficult for her to speak," noted Del, who wept herself at the sight of her stricken friend. Three days passed before Cornelia was able to write to her mother.

December 30, 1942

Dearest,

My mind has been in such turmoil and my heart has been so torn that I haven't written. But my heart has been with you for I know you have suffered as acutely as I. I know also that in a sense you have lost Dad all over again, for it was his abiding love at Fortland that made our love possible.

It seems as incredible to me that Fortland is gone as that black would change to white. No one knew how deeply I loved it, how many of my ideals and dreams were cradled there. It possessed for me all the magic of my childhood, all the laughter of my youth, all the gaiety and sunshine that has been my life.

It was infinitely more than a house or even a home to me. It was a way of life, and it was exactly for that way of life that my effort in this war was dedicated.

It was as alive to me as you, and in its passing I feel that part of my life has gone also. It represented dignity and graciousness, the beauty of family relationships, the strength of understanding and tolerance and a tranquillity that I shall never know again.

It was part of my strength and part of my integrity. Wherever I have been, whatever lands my eyes have beheld, the white columns of Fortland were always in my heart, a place of refuge and return.

The thought that we shall never again see morning sun slant thru the dining room window, that never again will we see the curtain billowing in the cool quiet morning air on the Angel's landing, that no longer will we sit in front of the fire with friends, that never again will we welcome people to the terrace in the afternoon's drowsy peace for a drink, that never ever will we see Spring be gently on the front lawn thru the columns, that never will our family meet again within its walls, that these things have passed is beyond the understanding of my heart.

Now there will be no wedding supper for one or either of Fortland's daughters within its walls—all the things I expected to be there long after my own death are utterly and cleanly gone. It is thin comfort to tell myself that I have the memory of it for always, that it will always and forever be in my heart. It is the closing of another circle for me; it is definitely and irrevocably the end of my youth. Now I will have no other strength but that which is within me, and that which is within me is a combination of you and Dad and Fortland and all the people who have touched my life and my heart.

My mind jumped to such scattered things, the lost and gone forever-ness of my diaries and the feeling it is no longer worthwhile to keep one, the burning of books which seems the same as human suffering, the loss of that *Madonna with a*

Lily, the loss of your rings and linen and silver, the loss of my bonds, whiskey, and those lovely Chinese underthings I almost brought back with me, and my Hollywood slacks, my skis and ski clothes, your letters and photographs, and the tiny things which mean so much. Not a very coherent list but neither is one's mind coherent. . . .

I am about to lead a flight to Texas which will, weather permitting, bring me thru Nashville. My transfer to Long Beach [California] is official but won't take place for three or four weeks. When it does, I think I can manage a few days in Nashville with you.

The entire McCain family gave me presents. Mrs. Mc gave me 3 pairs of nylons which are, of course, jewels without price. Bill gave me a gold bracelet which is lovely but

The rest of the letter is missing. A family story holds that Mrs. Fort was upset enough about what Cornelia had written regarding her relationship with Bill to destroy it.

Sixteen

As devastated as she was by the destruction of Fortland, Cornelia knew she was surrounded by women who had themselves known much tragedy. Because of her natural reserve, she might not have taken full advantage of their empathy, but the other WAFS understood her loss, and several had been through worse. Betty's four-year-old had died shortly before she joined the WAFS. Just a month before Fortland burned, Gertrude Meserve's twin brother had been one of 491 people killed when a fire roared through Boston's Coconut Grove nightclub. A few years earlier, Florene Miller's father and brother had been killed in a plane crash.

The women did not have time to stop and mourn; there was work to do. Until her transfer to Long Beach, Cornelia made a point of logging as much time on the Link Trainer as possible. The Link offered her the chance to prepare herself for new planes, routes, and flying conditions and to take her mind off the devastating loss of her home and so much of her personal history. The WAFS would use their downtime—and a spate of gloomy weather would assure them of that—to prepare for the move.

On the twenty-eighth, six of the WAFS received orders to take L4-Bs to Greenville, S.C., but after a day-long rain their departure was delayed until the next day. Nancy arrived late in the afternoon, and the group met at the officers' club, going back to BOQ 14 for what Betty called "a much-needed bull session." The weather remained miserable on the twenty-ninth, and the trip to Lock Haven was again delayed. BOQ 14, Betty wrote in her diary, was "an ocean of mud." That evening, the WAFS had a picnic lunch in the barracks, and Nancy, Betty, Cornelia, and Helen Mary did some brainstorming about the transfers that would split them up. They discussed which planes would be ferried from each of the new bases, which WAFS were qualified on each of them, and who might be sent with best effect to which base.

On the thirtieth, with the weather still bad, the WAFS learned that in the future all L4-Bs would be shipped rather than flown. When the weather cleared, they would not be heading to Lock Haven after all; they would go instead to the Hagerstown Fairchild factory to pick up PT-19s. In the dead of winter, they would be delivering the plane that most exposed them to the weather. Cubs, at least, had closed cockpits, which offered some shielding from the wind, if not from the cold. The Fairchilds were open to everything.

Colonel Baker joined Nancy, Betty, Cornelia, and Helen Mary for cocktails and dinner that evening and took them to his home for a nightcap. As they talked about the WAFS' future, Colonel Baker told Betty that within thirty days she would be flying a P-47, the big high-powered pursuit plane being built at the Republic factory on Long Island. Betty, Nancy, and the others had been looking wistfully at the P-47s on the flight line, hoping their chance at the big fighters would come.

"He was quite serious," Betty noted in her diary, "so I'm going to Daddy [her husband, Bud] to make me up some rudder extensions." One of the test pilots at Grumman was a man no bigger than Betty, and he had made himself a set of wooden blocks that slipped over his shoes to help him reach the rudders on the bigger planes. Once Betty got hers, she would carry them with her throughout her ferrying career.

On New Year's Eve, Nancy Love left for Dallas, leaving Betty as commander of the WAFS at the 2nd Ferrying Group. The women knew an era—brief though it was—was ending. The woman who had founded the WAFS, who had guided Cornelia and the rest through the program's infancy, whose calm sense of purpose had been such a stabilizing factor, would no longer be there.

During the first days of January 1943, the WAFS endured bad weather and ground school classes and talked a great deal about the future. Florene Miller, Helen Richards, Dorothy Scott, and November arrival Opal "Betsy" Ferguson were leaving to join Nancy Love in Dallas, home of the 5th Ferrying Group. Two weeks later, Barbara Poole, Del Scharr, Barbara Donahue, Phyllis Burchfield, and latecomer Katherine Thompson would head to the 3rd at Romulus. Quarters would not be ready at the 6th Ferrying Group in Long Beach until February 15, but B.J. would leave within days to oversee preparations for the other WAFS headed there: Cornelia, Bernice Batten, Evelyn Sharp, and Barbara Towne. As the exodus from New Castle began, a new pilot, Catherine "Sis" Bernheim, checked in and became part of the group.

On January 6, there were three accidents involving male pilots from the 2nd Ferrying Group, and there were two more on January 7. Betty wrote, "All hell has broken loose at headquarters," but the WAFS, given their well-established safety record, were not affected.

Cornelia, her mind still on Fortland, wrote to her mother on the afternoon of the seventh:

I'm still dazed. Having not seen the remains of Fortland I find it hard to picture it as gone. I want to help you in any way I can. Would you like me to try to list contents of the rooms & in so doing I might remember something you forgot.

Every once in a while I remember something else, like my favorite yellow coat, and realization prickles my spine. It is utterly & forever gone.

I hope with all my heart you will sell Fortland now. Aside from the farm which all of us loved in different, various ways, the real character of the place was Fortland itself. We would all have made sacrifices to have kept it but the farm is a drain, not only of your money, but what is more important, of your time & energy. As none of us could bear to rebuild where Fortland was & can never be again, the farm can have no substantial reason for remaining in your possession.

We could either build after the war or buy some house in the country, for I know you love gardens & country life as I do. You don't need so much land, however.

Cornelia did her best to offer her mother advice on friends who could help and concluded, "Poor Mother, I wish I could be with you."

That evening, Betty and Cornelia went to the Hotel du Pont for supper to celebrate Betty's birthday, getting back to base around ten-fifteen. The weather turned colder overnight, and on January 8 the field was closed because of ice on the runway. That evening, the entire base was ordered to see an installment of *Why We Fight*, a Frank Capra–directed documentary that outlined the reasons for U.S. entry into the war. Afterward, the WAFS returned to the BOQ and Betty called the doctor about Cornelia, who had been battling a cold or flu for days.

Cornelia's illness may well have been symptomatic of the stresses she was under. Her life demanded every bit of the strength and stamina she possessed. She was also battling private obstacles— pressure from Bill McCain to marry, the destruction of her home and possessions, and, most recently, the urgings of her family that she leave the WAFS.

Dudley had written Mrs. Fort that Cornelia was under tremendous strain and should resign. Ever the worrier, he had told Cornelia the same thing. "You've done enough for the country," he said. Instead, Cornelia arranged for leave and joined her mother for a week in Florida. A family story holds that Cornelia had what amounted to a breakdown and that the trip provided the time she needed to recover. There is no evidence, though, that such was the case, although it is clear Cornelia welcomed the break and the opportunity to be with her mother. Between January 22 and 27 they were at the Seacrest Hotel in Delray, Florida, and spent time in Miami Beach.

Cornelia's February 4 letter to her mother, who had stopped to visit Dudley on her way home to Nashville, hardly reflects the mindset of someone who has recently undergone a breakdown. It opened as follows:

Dearest,

Dudley wrote that they loved having you. I hope you had fun. I can't begin to tell you how much I loved being with you. It was wonderful fun and something we must try again. For instance, South America. I appreciate your going with me more than I can say.

Cornelia returned from south Florida to the kind of miserable weather the base had faced for months. Snow and sleet closed the field on Thursday, January 28, and the WAFS attended lectures as part of their continuing ground school. Even getting to classes was difficult. "It was some job navigating on foot into the teeth of the storm," Betty wrote in her diary. The field was finally opened on Monday, but the wind was still so strong that only the bigger planes were allowed to fly. During a brief window of good weather that week, the field was crowded with planes going up as men and women sought to make up for lost time, in many cases checking out in bigger planes. By Thursday, February 4, though, the bad weather was back. As rain and fog closed the runway yet again, Cornelia sat down and wrote to her mother.

"Not a word from McCain," she wrote. "He must really have the sulks. I returned the bracelet & felt like a damn fool. I'm sure he doesn't want it back but I guess it is better."

She followed with another letter the next day, her birthday. "I'm a birthday girl & never felt less so. I feel about 104 instead of 24." The loss of Fortland, her problems with Bill, and the breakup of the original WAFS unit were all weighing on her. Still, she looked to lift her spirits with her mother's birthday gift. "The slip is breathtaking," she told her. "I'll feel as flossy as Mae West when I put it under my uniform."

The rain and fog continued, and Sunday was so windy that nothing smaller than B-26s or P-47s could fly. That day, Cornelia sat down with a legal pad and, in longhand, began to write her own history as a flyer. Cornelia had always had a sense of herself as part of something bigger. She was a proud member of her storied family, and she was thrilled now with the unprecedented opportunity she had to serve the country she loved so much. She had also been driven since childhood to record her thoughts, from the homely details of day-to-day existence to the deepest stirrings of her soul. With her move to Long Beach just days away, she looked back on her time in Delaware, grateful both for the camaraderie and for the chance to live her dream.

> All of us realized what a terrific spot we were on and drew closer together as a result. I've seen everything now, for I have seen the miracle of women working together in cooperation and friendliness. For we knew that on our efforts hung the fate, at least in any military form of endeavor, of not us alone but of untold future women pilots. . . .
>
> I for one am so profoundly grateful that my one talent, my only knowledge, flying, happens to be of use to my country when it is needed. That's all the luck I ever hope to have.

Cornelia's transfer to Long Beach came through as she and six other WAFS delivered P-26s from Hagerstown over Niagara Falls to Toronto. They returned on the eleventh, a rainy Thursday that was to be Cornelia's last full day on the base. She wangled one day's leave en route to Long Beach, wired her mother that she would use it to visit Nashville, and prepared for the trip.

That evening, the remaining WAFS gave a going-away cocktail party for Cornelia, Barbara Towne, and Evelyn Sharp. The group went to the officers' mess for a steak dinner and then to the theater to watch *Commandos Strike at Dawn* with Paul Muni and Lillian Gish. The film was a fitting close to Cornelia's tenure at New Castle, depicting as it did the struggle of Norwegian villagers against the Nazi invaders. Cornelia's love of freedom and hatred of tyranny were basic principles, as much a part of her Fort heritage as her lanky frame. They had inspired her as an editorial writer at Sarah Lawrence, and she was willing to put her very life on the line for them now.

Seventeen

The skies were a deep clear blue in Wilmington Friday as Cornelia, Barbara, and Evelyn left for Long Beach. Cornelia found the weather much different in her hometown. She arrived in Nashville Friday evening, and on Saturday she went foxhunting in a snowstorm. After spending the evening with her mother, she boarded a plane early Sunday for the remainder of the trip.

Despite the fact that it was sunny and hot, Long Beach quickly provided the WAFS with a sense of déjà vu: As had been the case in New Castle, their barracks weren't ready. "Apparently," Cornelia wrote her mother, "they hadn't done a thing about quarters for us until Sat. afternoon when they emptied a hospital ward [the women were told it had been a psychiatric ward] and I do mean emptied. When I arrived there wasn't a chair, a bed, a towel, or anything. Just a 60-foot-long gaping room." Cornelia and the others checked into the downtown Villa Riviera Hotel and headed for the beach. "There in a nutshell is the miracle of aviation; foxhunting one day in a blizzard & lying on a beach 3,000 miles away the next," she wrote.

By midweek they were back in their makeshift barracks, which had much in common with BOQ 14: the same lack of wallboard, with two-by-fours exposed on the walls, and the same chests of drawers and army cots. This time, though, the WAFS had their cots together in a row along one wall. Again, they quickly began to add their personal touches, hanging photos and spreading rugs.

"The most noticeable difference between New Castle and here, aside from the weather, is the happy expressions on all the faces. People stare at us as we knew they would, but they are friendly stares. Pilots say 'Welcome' and seem to mean it." As always, Cornelia ran into a number of old friends, including Second Lieutenant Bill Lacy ("the one who sailed his little boat to Honolulu and spent last Easter at Fortland").

The 6th Ferrying Group had been organized at the Long Beach Municipal Airport in August 1941 to ferry planes from Southern California's aircraft manufacturers. The facility, now called Long Beach Army Air Field, offered the WAFS more than just good weather. For one thing, the officers' club was "pretty glamorous—sprinkled with movie stars and silver chafing dishes filled with fried oysters and cheese." The post band was probably the country's best; many musicians from the most popular big bands had been drafted, and a good percentage of them were at Long Beach.

More important, there was instant access to bigger and better planes than the WAFS had ever been allowed inside at New Castle. "We checked out in BT-13s the very first morning," Cornelia told her mother. "They are the biggest planes any of us have flown really and truly alone (450 horsepower)."

Still, the WAFS were impressive in their Long Beach debuts. "We first three girls soloed the planes in the minimum allowable time and did a fine job, a fact which was naturally gratifying." She added:

> Yesterday we went on an Instrument Flight & I was able
> to apply the knowledge I've gained in the Link Trainer at
> Wilmington. It was also gratifying to get on one of the most

complicated Radio Range Systems (there are seven Range Stations overlapping within a radius of 50 miles) in the country & fly by radio from one to another with sureness & certainty—in a twin-engined airplane I'd never flown before. I'm so glad I worked hard on it at NCAAB. I really feel as if I'm a 500% better pilot than I was last fall. And besides, the rewards of my thirst for knowledge have always been a source of pleasure to me. To ache for knowledge, work for it, & then see the results is the most wonderful thing I know.

I think we will be very happy here. If things continue to move as fast as they have in the first few days, I know we will be.

They would continue to do so. Cornelia spoke with base commander Colonel Ralph E. Spake the day she checked out in the BT-13. "Reluctantly, he told me that he had had excellent reports on all of us," she told her mother, "and he added that the men who had given him the reports were tough men to please."

The WAFS themselves would be led by B.J. Erickson, the twenty-two-year-old pilot who had impressed Nancy with her leadership, organizational ability, and record-keeping skills at New Castle. Also, B.J. had grown very close to Betty Gillies on missions they had flown together in PT-19s—missions that found them weathered in for extended periods. They were among the oldest and youngest of the WAFS and began referring to each other as "Mother" and "Daughter." B.J. had a terrific reputation as a flyer, and her closeness with Betty no doubt helped spur the decision to name her squadron commander.

Cornelia supported the choice enthusiastically, saying she had little interest in the position herself. "Whoever gets the job will have a lot of desk work and a certain amount of post politics to cope with," she wrote her mother. "Neither one appeals to me."

The group would await orders in the Pilots' Loft, a room on the second floor of a barracks building. It was a ten-minute walk across the parade grounds and Spring Street, then through a gate and up the stairs. The Loft had a lunch counter and tables and chairs where the pilots would play cards or otherwise kill time after arriving at 8 A.M.

They got to work almost immediately, checking out in new planes and going on ferrying runs. Long Beach handled a wide variety of aircraft, and the WAFS knew they would get the chance to fly many of them. For the moment, they were mostly ferrying the BT-13 and the BT-15, essentially the same plane with a different engine.

The BT-13, a basic trainer manufactured by Vultee Aircraft of nearby Downey, California, was bigger and more powerful than anything the five women had previously flown, and it seemed like a giant step up. It was a two-seater, 29 feet long with a 42-foot wingspan, and it cruised at 140 mph. It had low wings, an enclosed canopy that pilots sometimes slid open on hot days to catch the wind, and a 450-horsepower engine; it even had a radio. Its nickname was the "Vultee Vibrator" because it shuddered and rattled violently when a pilot tried to bring it out of a spin, a feat which, given the plane's size, took a good 2,000 feet of altitude. It was also a plane in which they quickly learned to hang on to their maps. Drop one, and it could easily slide through slats on the floor into the belly of the aircraft.

On Thursday, February 18, Cornelia was part of a six-plane mission to Love Field in Dallas. She and B.J. flew BT-13s while

Barbara, Evelyn, Bill Lacy, and Second Lieutenant Jack Browning flew BT-15s. On February 22, Cornelia wrote to her mother about the trip. It was one of the rare letters she typed.

Mother dear,

We have completed our first mission [already]. It was the pleasantest trip of any we have had, which speaks well for our new post. Of course the reason for this was the airplane, which we loved, which had a delightful radio to take us blithely across the desert, and the weather, which was unbelievable.

And of all the coincidences which will never happen again was the fact that Bill Lacy went out with us on the same orders. We spent the first night in Palm Springs, where the officers' club is a guest ranch complete with swimming pool. The moon was full and the desert smelled of all the wonderful flowers I ever imagined. That was one of the times when I knew clearly the reason for my love of flying, why I wouldn't change jobs for anything else in the world. The reasons are many. I know them in the beauty I see, in the freedom of the air, in the pride of skill and the joy of self-sufficiency.

The next day we flew to Phoenix for lunch and to El Paso for the night. Bill and I went to Juarez, Mexico, which is right across the border, for dinner. It is a typical border town: touristy, full of souvenir shops, and trashy beyond belief. But it was fun for once. We had dinner in the fanciest place there, which had Mexican music and castanet players and guitar-playing sombrero-ed men. I was in bed by 10 so you can see the "gaiety" of ferry pilots on trips.

The desert is a very safe place to fly across for you could land anywhere, but it would also be a very easy place to get lost in, for the stretches of sand and space are incredible. It is the most nothing I have ever seen. This was the first time I ever flew with a superb radio and I have discovered a new world. All the Link work I did in Wilmington stood me in good stead. I simply tuned in on Tucson when I left Phoenix and flew the beam directly to the Tucson airport, where I tuned in on the next station and so on. All the worries of navigation are reduced to one worry and that is that your radio will go dead.

From El Paso we flew to Big Spring, Texas, and on into Dallas, where we delivered the planes. The distance was 1,304 miles, twice what it was from Wilmington to Nashville, and I flew this in nine hours total or a day and a half instead of a week. I was making good a speed of 180 instead of 60.

If I don't write often here it will be because I am so busy. It is indeed refreshing to see one place in the Army run well and efficiently.

If the WAFS had been lulled into any sense of complacency by the warm welcome they'd received from the pilots, their first encounter with the pilots' wives, on February 23, quickly changed that. Cornelia wrote her mother:

Today we went perforce to the bi-monthly luncheon at the officers' club, of officers' wives. It was the most desperate ordeal I ever saw. Talk about being stared at & appraised & in a decidedly unfriendly fashion. Whew! They are in a frenzy of jealousy that we will co-pilot with their husbands. Of all the damned, stupid, female rot!

Col. Spake sent his Deputy to make a speech—which had a dual purpose. Theoretically it was a speech of welcome for us; actually, it was an announcement to the wives that they need not worry, that no "mixed operations orders" would be issued, i.e., no man & girl as pilot & co-pilot.

And can you believe it, the rude women applauded right in front of us! I was so livid at an exhibition whose equal I had never seen that I got up & walked out, whereupon the other girls followed me. I hope [the wives] had the grace to be ashamed of their rudeness, if not their feelings.

Col. Spake, however firm he is on that subject, is otherwise very kind & obviously very proud of us. He has promised us fabulous things & soon, & he is noted for being a man of his word. He was delighted at our delivering to Dallas in such speed & safety. He was nearly purring this morning.

From the beginning, the WAFS would be the objects of jealousy and suspicion from the wives, but they were far too busy to worry about it. There was little time to do anything but get to work. They were doing the same job as the men, ferrying expensive, complex equipment around the country, and they knew they were needed. Moreover, despite the "mixed orders" ban, Long Beach's attitude toward mixed "flights"—those with WAFS and male officers in separate planes on the same trips—was much more liberal than it had been at New Castle. While there had been occasional mixed flights back east, the WAFS' trips to pick up planes were often timed to make sure there would be no men beginning ferrying trips concurrently. That would not be the situation in California.

Many of their new male colleages were taken with both the women and their skills.

"We really respected them very much," said Flight Officer John C. Irving, who was stationed at Long Beach. "We kind of fought for the opportunity to fly with them because they were such nice gals." The respect grew out of the fact that the WAFS had much more flying time than many of the men, most of whom had just come out of flight school. Others, though, did not have such positive attitudes. "A lot of the fellows were ninety-day wonders," said Barbara Poole. "They had nothing in flying time but thought they were far superior to us."

Overall, the treatment the women would receive in Long Beach was good, as it had been in Wilmington; the men, after all, were happy to have women on the base, even if many initially doubted the WAFS' skills. On the road, attitudes varied. Some of the WAFS experienced very little in the way of inappropriate behavior. For others, flying talk fairly often led to come-ons.

"On trips we stayed clear of the guys," said Teresa. "They sounded like a broken record: 'I might not come back.' They would try to impress us by talking about the power and might of the aircraft they could fly. Anything to get you into the sack."

In general, though, the attitude of the male pilots wasn't of much interest to Cornelia. It was the flying that captured her imagination, and she was ecstatic at the amount of it available to her in Long Beach. Too much of her life at New Castle had involved waiting. Early on, she dropped her mother a postcard from

Palm Springs: "We are eastbound in BT-13's. Spending the afternoon & night here. Wow! It is lovely. Hot desert sun. What a good post we were transferred to. More action in 5 days than in 5 months at NCAAB."

Cornelia learned quickly one of the odder side effects of desert flying. The WAFS flew mostly west to east, often in open-cockpit planes, and they sometimes experienced sunburn on the south-facing cheek—a flyer might come off a trip with the right side of her face bright red except for a big white spot left around her right eye by her goggles.

With the little free time they had available, the WAFS tried to carve out social lives, and the officers' club, with its top-drawer band, was again a prime source of diversion. There was also bowling and the base theater, and, as always, Cornelia had friends in the region. She was especially drawn to Peter and Ruth Davis, whom she had known in Nashville, where his father was chairman of the board of First American National Bank. In fact, Cornelia's first diary entry, nearly two months after the burning of Fortland and the loss of her other diaries and books, recorded a visit to their Pasadena home on February 22. She described them in her diary and in her letters.

They are a young couple who braved all kinds of threats and disapproval to get married and who are without doubt the happiest couple I ever saw anywhere. They are so in love after three years that it is heartwarming to be with them, and that plus the fact that they love me as much as I love them makes it a very happy place to go. It is a darling low rambling white-brick house with patio (for steak broiling), outside closet for skis, etc., badminton court, beam ceilings, fireplaces, & the greatest profusion of landscaping & horticulture I ever witnessed. During the one nite & morning I was there we used limes from their trees in rum Collins, avocados in salad, figs and dates for dessert, homegrown orange juice, & camellias for my hair. They also have lemon, guava, strawberries, hibiscus, orchids, peaches, & more than is believable. I never saw such a glamorous, bread-fruit kind of life.

They want me to come & live with them, which I would dearly love to do, but I'm afraid it would be difficult as to trans-portation. Without a car here you are more helpless than any-where else in the country. Pasadena might as well be 528 miles instead of 28. I may get a car and I may spend many nites with them, but living 28 miles away from the post would be diffi-cult when I came in at 3 A.M. from trips, etc.

Besides making overnight stays difficult, the WAFS' hectic schedules had another unexpected effect. Cornelia and the others found that it was more difficult to keep up with the war and the world situation than it had been before they joined the squad-ron. The WAFS had fallen into a busy routine. They would come back off a mission, take care of their paperwork, fall into bed, and then get up and very likely pick up another set of orders that morning.

"We were in our own little world," said B.J., "and the details of the war often passed us by. We could pick up a newspaper once in a while, and we had radio and the newsreels, but we were gone ninety percent of the time, sleeping in hotels or waiting in rail-road stations, and we weren't really aware of all that the war entailed. I don't think any of us understood it all. It was just too big. . . . We just knew how important it was for those airplanes to get where they had to go."

On Wednesday, February 24, Cornelia, B.J., and Barbara received orders to deliver BT-15s to the San Antonio Air Depot for delivery to Chilean pilots. They stayed that night in Palm Springs, where they had, according to Cornelia's diary, "a swim, drink & steak at the Officers' Ranch & a mild circuit with innumerable ferry pilots. Without doubt the best R.O.N. [remained overnight] in the USA."

On Thursday they flew on to Tucson and then into El Paso, where they stayed overnight. Friday they delivered the planes and Cornelia went sightseeing in San Antonio, seeing the Alamo with Lieutenant Bert Peterson and joining friends for cocktails, followed by dinner at La Fonda, where Cornelia enjoyed "the only Mex. food I've ever been able to swallow. . . . What a fun trip!"

Saturday, Cornelia was back in Long Beach in time to welcome Nancy Love, who flew in from Dallas. Colonel Spake had promised the WAFS "fabulous things," and this trip was a major step toward making good on that pledge. The WAFS had already begun flying larger planes, and that afternoon Nancy became one of only a handful of flyers and the first woman to fly the P-51 Mustang, the 400-mph "Cadillac of the Air," a pursuit plane that would not even be ready for combat for months. The other WAFS had been promised that they too would fly the P-51 after delivering five BTs. Nancy then checked out in a C-47 cargo plane, the military version of the Douglas DC-3. "What a great day for the females," Cornelia wrote. In celebration, she and Nancy went to that evening's officers' club dance, but, said Cornelia, "the smoke drove us home early." The following night the two went back to the club for dinner.

On Monday, March 1, Cornelia, Barbara, and Evelyn were ordered to fly BT-15s to Love Field as part of a trip involving about two dozen BT-13s and BT-15s. That night, after a swim and dinner in Palm Springs, she and the others treated themselves to "a ramble around, listening to some fancy piano playing."

Some of the flying across the desert had already become routine.

"I know the route to Dallas so well now I've cut a groove in the sky," she wrote Johnny Koons, whom she had once dated. "I only used my radio 30 minutes out of 10 hrs. flying, and that for calling in to stations." Cornelia began using the time aloft to catch up on her correspondence. Using stationery from the Royal Palms, she wrote her mother Tuesday. "I'm on my third BT-13 trip & writing this epistle two miles above the desert between Tucson and El Paso." She discussed recent developments, including Nancy's trailblazing work in the larger planes. "Those airplanes should be substantial enough to please you. After a Cub they look like flying houses to me."

As she had always done, Cornelia enclosed a $50 check, apparently for two months' rent on her room at Fortland, even though the mansion was no longer there. It was not income her mother needed. Busy as ever with her outside activities, Mrs. Fort was well provided for by the income from her deceased husband's holdings. "These checks just keep coming in," she told a friend, who once noticed that many often lay uncashed for long periods.

There was nothing routine about the next leg of Cornelia's trip. After leaving El Paso for Dallas, she "had terrible carburetor ice over Guadalupe Pass—a very unhealthy place for ice. Limped into Midland, an army base." As usual, Cornelia knew people on the base and in the area. She stayed with friends and spent the next afternoon in Dallas watching *Casablanca* and visiting Neiman-Marcus. Back in Long Beach, she joined Nancy and several other friends for dinner at a club called Leilani. "A very attractive place much like Trader Vic's," she wrote. "The tapa-covered walls, Hawaiian scenes, and real Hawaiian music made me suddenly and acutely homesick for the islands. Such a lost, beautiful world."

Eighteen

New flying opportunities became a hot topic among the WAFS. Betty, as promised, became the first woman to fly the P-47 Thunderbolt, and Nancy knew there was more to come for all of them. She was qualified on more than a dozen types of aircraft, most of them manufactured in Southern California, and she knew Long Beach would offer many more opportunities than Dallas. On March 3, she requested a transfer to the 6th Ferrying Group; it was approved eight days later. B.J. was taking every flight she could get as well, and she and Nancy teamed up on March 5 to fly a twin-engine C-47 cargo plane from Long Beach to Memphis.

If they thought their climb toward bigger planes would suddenly get easy, though, the women were mistaken. There was still a great deal of resistance to such a move, and March 17 orders from Colonel Tunner's office limited the WAFS to single-engine planes and said the women were not to fly bombers, even as co-pilots, despite their praiseworthy safety and efficiency records.

For the time being, Cornelia took advantage of the downtime after the Dallas flight to do some socializing, taking the bus to Los Angeles for lunch with a friend. She told her mother:

> It was good for my morale to get dressed in civilian
> clothes, go to the very elegant Town House for lunch in the
> Cape Cod Room. Even to have a cocktail, avocado stuffed

with crabmeat & French pastry, was like prewar excitement. I felt like a lady instead of a WAFS.

Then I went to Pasadena to be with Ruth & Peter for the nite. It was so damn pleasant to sit in a quiet, well-ordered, gracious house with friends. They are always exceedingly heart-warming. They love me just as much as I love them.

Cornelia

Cornelia finally decided to put an end to the isolation imposed by her lack of a car. On Tuesday, March 9, she bought a gray 1941 Chevrolet convertible with a radio and red leather upholstery from a Lieutenant Moore. It was, she told her mother, "a dream car this time instead of a junk heap. I felt so helpless without one & distances are so tremendous out here. . . . It will be wonderful fun this summer to put the top down." Conscious too of the real dangers of her job, she added, "If anything should happen to me—which I don't think will—I want Louise to have the car."

Later, on March 16, she wrote her mother:

Dearest

The weather has been consistently bad & altho I've been on orders 5 days, I still haven't gone anywhere. My little car has already been a joy especially with its top down & the Cal. sun pouring in.

I spent last Fri. nite with Ruth and Peter. After dinner we lay on the floor in front of a fire & toasted marshmallows and chatted way into the night.

Sunday we were dismissed early so one of the girls & 2 pilots and I drove down to Laguna Beach to a very famous old inn, the Victor Hugo. It is high on a bluff over the ocean with flowers growing up & down the slopes. We sat in a glass-enclosed room all the late part of the afternoon & watched the sun on the water. That such an attractive place should also have out of this-world food was too much to expect. Avocado cocktail, sweetbreads in a wine & cream sauce, & French pastry.

Will you send the blue denim shorts, the fancy yellow dress, one or two chambray dresses, the brown shorts, the 3-piece bathing suit (shirt, bra, & pants from Hawaii) along with the shoe ration stamp.

And please write more often. I miss you so much.

Love

C—

P.S. Oh, joy! Nancy is being transferred here.

Besides missing her mother, Cornelia apparently hungered for more of a relationship with Johnny Koons, who was stationed in the Pacific but about whom nothing else is known. Cornelia never mentioned him, either to her friends in Nashville or to the other WAFS, and he is known primarily from a letter which came back to Cornelia as undeliverable. It is as passionate as it is mysterious. She wrote in part:

Oh, Johnny, when is the day coming that you and I can meet like normal people and not on railroad station platforms or between planes or at a hotel in a strange city or among strangers? When can we put the top down on my little buggy and drive out in the country for dinner at a little inn and stay there a week if we like? When will we be able to ride horses thru the fields of Fortland with Kevin running with us? Write to me. I miss you so much sometimes I can hardly stand it.

Love,

Cornelia

Still, Cornelia was doing work she loved, she had good friends nearby, and she felt both fulfilled and self-sufficient. She told her brother Garth, "I love everything about the post, the people, the planes, & my gray convertible."

Cornelia was to deliver a BT-13 to Love Field in Dallas for ultimate use in flight training. There were, in fact, a number of BT-13s ready for delivery, and all five of the Long Beach WAFS were photographed with one for a story to appear in *Air-Age* magazine the following August. Cornelia, Evelyn, and B.J. hoisted themselves onto the right wing of one of the big planes for the photo, while Barbara and Bernice stationed themselves at either end.

Pilots from Long Beach kept a steady stream of BT-13s and BT-15s headed for Dallas early in 1943 for delivery to bases all over the South and Southwest. Men and women frequently flew joint missions, although they were never in the same planes. All flight orders were individual, but if several pilots had the same destination, they might well take off as a group. Even then, in many cases, the pilots would often lose sight of each other quickly and for the duration of the trip. Sometimes, though, they would fly in loose formation, keeping each other in sight as the WAFS had to do in Wilmington when they were flying tiny planes with no radios. Tight formation, however, with pilots sitting just off each other's wings, was forbidden for the WAFS; they had not been trained for it and had no experience.

There was another very practical reason for the ban on tight formation: A percentage of the men flying these missions were young, inexperienced, and sometimes reckless, and the presence of women could bring out the worst in them. All the WAFS experienced or heard of incidents in which male pilots, showing off or attempting to frighten the women, would play fighter-pilot, rolling and weaving near them, buzzing them or coming suddenly alongside, so the women generally kept a wary eye on them. Still, the WAFS, especially as they grew more comfortable in their role, often ignored the rule.

"We used to fly formation all the time," said Betty Guild, Cornelia's old Honolulu friend, who went on to graduate from Jackie Cochran's program and fly out of Long Beach. "The army frowned on it, but we did it."

Cornelia, in the costliest decision of her life, would do it too.

Nineteen

The flight to Dallas took Cornelia back over the same long open stretch of desert with which she had become so familiar. She was, after just a few weeks, much more relaxed about the route. She took off at 9 A.M. on Sunday, March 21, from Tucson and landed at 12:45 in Midland to refuel. She chatted at the airport snack bar with a group of male pilots from Long Beach who were also headed to Dallas, and, after a while, the conversation turned to formation flying. Some of the pilots had flown formation while in training, although they too were forbidden to do so while on ferrying missions. Like the WAFS, they were to maintain a 500-foot distance from anything in the sky. But over country this remote, it might be fun to practice.

"My recollection," said Louis A. Biggio, a second lieutenant in the airport group, "is that Cornelia had never done that, and she said, 'I'd like to try it.' She was a little hesitant. I don't re- member whether we tried to talk her into it." The other pilots told her she could simply fly straight and level—that they would fly on her wing. Another lieutenant, Frank F. Wiggins, said he wanted no part of it and would see them in Dallas. The rest agreed to meet in the air.

To save time, the six male pilots signed out their ships on flight plans filed by Wiggins and Second Lieutenant Curtis R. Hovde. The flight included Cornelia, Biggio, Hovde, Wiggins, First Lieutenant Bruce Calkins, and flight officers John C. Irving and Frank Stamme Jr. They took off at 2:37 P.M. and met at 7,000 feet over the rugged West Texas mesas for the two-hour flight. Cornelia brought her air speed to 140 miles per hour, as did the others.

"We were headed eastward, flying formation," said Biggio, "changing position sometimes, switching around, from right wing to left wing. We weren't any too close—just flying the way we would in training. It was fun. We were young and full of vinegar, and none of us ever considered the possible consequences."

Irving confirmed that they were flying formation—"just practicing, I guess"—noting that this was a group of young pilots out of flight school just ninety days. "We were very, very young and very inexperienced," he said.

The group flew south of Sweetwater at about three-thirty, and Biggio had to make a position report. He pulled to the right of the main group to check his radio facility chart, then looked to the left and saw the planes flown by Stamme and Cornelia flying extremely close together. Stamme had just turned twenty-three. He had entered flight school the previous April and had become a flight officer in December. He had 267 hours in the air, about a quarter of what Cornelia had, although he, like the others, had more experience in larger planes.

Over rough, hilly country about ten miles south of Merkel, Biggio saw Cornelia's plane "suddenly break off to the right as though on a snap roll."

Stamme told investigators, "I glanced to my right and rear, just in time to see the other plane off my right trailing edge. The ship seemed to be in a slight turn or skid, with the wing slightly tilted. The collision was unavoidable as far as my doing anything, even though my reaction was to pull up, causing [what I believe] to be her canopy to hit my right landing gear. In the split second that all this happened, I noticed the pilot of the other ship had her left arm raised as if to ward off a blow or shield her face from something. I never saw the pilot raise her arm; it was in that position when I first saw it."

What actually struck Stamme's landing gear was Cornelia's left wing, according to the AAF. The tip of that wing, which was made of wood—the other was entirely metal—snapped off, and the impact peeled six feet of the wing's leading edge toward the fuselage.

Biggio watched as Cornelia's plane spun slowly down until he lost sight of it beneath his wing. It rolled several times, went into an inverted dive, rotating slowly to the left, and slammed vertically into the ground. It plowed several feet into the red soil and never moved or caught fire. Most likely, said Second Lieutenant Warren L. Sparks, who investigated the crash, the engine was buried underground too quickly for the bulk of the fuel, which was in wing tanks, to ignite.

The initial impact with Stamme's plane had apparently knocked Cornelia unconscious or killed her instantly. She made no attempt to open the emergency latch on the hatch release and apparently did not try to right the plane. The plane was too badly mangled to tell if she had turned off the ignition following the collision, although the plane lost power almost immediately afterward.

Stamme had maintained control of his lightly damaged aircraft. He and Biggio circled at a very low altitude, as did two others. Biggio looked for smoke or flame, for any sign of a crash, and saw nothing. He concluded that Cornelia had pulled out of the spin, and he headed toward Dallas, as did all the others except Stamme. When he arrived, Biggio learned that Cornelia had crashed.

Stamme headed for nearby Abilene. "I made an emergency landing in the dirt next to the runway," he told investigators, "believing I had washed out my landing gear."

The Associated Press quoted unofficial sources in Abilene as saying witnesses saw two planes tip wings before Cornelia's went out of control. Nearby farmers heard the crash and came running to the site, a pasture two miles southeast of the little town of Nubia. When they arrived, the plane lay still and broken in the bright Texas sun.

Betty Joe Seymore, a fourteen-year-old from a nearby farm, saw scalp and hair in a tree not far from the plane—Cornelia's body had essentially exploded upon impact—and knew the pilot had been a woman. Another neighbor, H. H. Cargill, found an insignia pin and a piece of Cornelia's watch, which had been smashed flat. There were only 60 pounds of remains that could be collected to be shipped back to Nashville. Cornelia had weighed 140 pounds.

Mr. and Mrs. Clyde Latimer and Joe Seymore, Betty Joe's father, stood guard at the site until army personnel arrived.

Almost at once, rumors began circulating that Stamme had been hotdogging, trying to scare or impress Cornelia during the flight. Many of the WAFS had seen such actions from young male pilots. The story, reprinted in several books about the WAFS, was that Stamme had been showing off and that, in doing a roll over Cornelia's plane, his plane struck hers, causing the crash. There is no evidence that such a thing happened. It is known that they were flying closer together than was permitted, and that her wing struck his landing gear. Either could have made the split-second mental error that resulted in the collision—Stamme had less than 300 hours in the air, but Cornelia had precious little experience flying anything other than tiny planes. Once the collision took place, the wooden wing on Cornelia's plane helped assure it would be fatal.

B.J. Erickson, head of the Long Beach WAFS, said she believed the collision was accidental. "They were in two or three airplanes out there in the middle of nowhere trying to fly formation," she said. "I don't think there was anything malicious about it. I think it was a plain accident."

The army interviewed all the pilots in the air—none of whom discussed the fact that they had been flying formation—and all those who saw anything from the ground. The cause of the accident, the report said, was "100 percent judgment. Momentary lapse of mental efficiency. General lack of alertness, etc." It did not assign blame.

Cornelia, at twenty-four, became the first woman pilot to die on active duty in U.S. history.

Twenty

Mrs. Fort learned of Cornelia's death that night in a call from Cornelius A. Craig, grandfather of Cornelia's friend Elizabeth Craig and a cofounder of National Life. He had gotten the news from his nephew, a Texas newspaper publisher who heard the initial report of the crash. After telling Mrs. Fort by phone, Craig and Charles R. Clements, another cofounder of National Life and a close family friend, drove over to see her. Mrs. Fort later received a call from the base. The following morning, Colonel Spake wired her from Long Beach:

CONFIRMING THE TELEPHONE CONVERSATION OF MARCH 21 1943 IT IS MY SAD DUTY TO INFORM YOU OF THE DEATH OF YOUR DAUGHTER CORNELIA FORT ON SUNDAY MARCH 21 1943 NEAR MERKEL TEXAS. THE SYMPATHY OF THE ENTIRE PERSONNEL OF THE ARMY AIR FORCES SIXTH FERRYING GROUP IS EXTENDED TO YOU IN THE BEREAVEMENT OF YOUR DAUGHTER. REQUEST YOU NOTIFY THE COMMANDING OFFICER SIXTH FERRYING GROUP LONG BEACH ARMY AIR FIELD GOVERNMENT COLLECT AS TO DISPOSITION OF RE-MAINS. I ASSURE YOU THAT WE SHALL FOLLOW YOUR DESIRES AND AGAIN EXTEND OUR HEARTFELT SYMPATHIES.

The casket was sealed and draped with a flag in Abilene, and Cornelia's remains were shipped Tuesday morning on the Sunshine Special from Abilene to Memphis, where the train was met by an escort from the Memphis airfield. From there, it continued to Nashville, where Cornelia's body arrived at Rufus's house Wednesday afternoon. Mrs. Fort received friends and family and sat up with the casket overnight.

"If she had listened to me," she told people, "it would have never happened." Mrs. Fort had never wanted Cornelia to fly on Sunday, the day this accident, like Pearl Harbor, had taken place.

Bernice Batten had the cot next to Cornelia's in the barracks at Long Beach, and they shared a makeshift wardrobe. She heard on the way back to Long Beach from a mission that Cornelia had been killed. Bernice got back to the barracks, exhausted, to find that a big cardboard box filled with Cornelia's mangled clothing had been left on her cot.

Nancy Love and B.J. went to Nashville for the funeral, arriving at 5:30 A.M. on Thursday, March 25. At 8:30, after finding a hotel, they called Mrs. Fort, who had been expecting them. When they arrived at Mrs. Fort's home at 10 A.M., the family wanted to hear everything the two women knew, which wasn't much. They had been told very little about the accident.

Christ Episcopal Church was filled with many of the state's most prominent citizens, most of whom were friends of the family, as the 3 P.M. service got under way. More than two hundred floral arrangements, including yellow roses and orchids from Governor Prentice Cooper, filled the chancel and later surrounded the gravesite. Clen Robertson sent a wreath that included calla lilies, common in wedding bouquets. Officiating with the church's rector was the Right Reverend E. P. Dandridge, bishop coadjutor of Tennessee. The pallbearers included some of National Life's top executives.

Nancy, B.J., and a Major Dunlap, who had flown to Nashville with them, led the processional up the church aisle. The officers of the 20th Ferrying Group from Berry Field were in attendance as well. Since Cornelia was a civilian, there was no military escort.

The graveside service at Mt. Olivet Cemetery lasted an hour, and Cornelia was buried next to her father, who had died almost exactly three years earlier. Cornelia's footstone would read KILLED IN THE SERVICE OF HER COUNTRY.

Telegrams poured in from all over the country, from friends of Cornelia and of the family, including the two men to whom Cornelia had been closest. "Impossible for me to believe the grandest girl I ever knew is gone," wrote Bill McCain from New York, "I will never forget her. My deepest sympathy to you." Clen Robertson, in Fort Benning, Georgia, wrote, "Cornelia had courage that would never turn back. It is hard to think of life without her. All my love and sympathy."

Throughout the WAFS, the young women who had lived and worked and flown with Cornelia were left to sort out their emotions.

"There was a terrific impact on us when she was killed," said B.J., who remembered wanting to strangle an officer who said, "Isn't that too bad. And she just bought a new car."

"It's a horrible thing to have happen," Evelyn Sharp wrote to her parents, on the day of Cornelia's funeral. "We still haven't sent her clothes home and everything is here just as she left it. Makes the barracks a little eerie at night. It is just a big room with six beds, and now it seems a little spooky. But her time must have been here."

On March 30, after returning to Long Beach, Nancy wrote to Mrs. Fort. "My feeling about the loss of Cornelia is hard to put into words," she said. "I can only say that I miss her terribly and loved her. She was a rare person. If there can be any comforting thought, it is that she died as she wanted to—in an army airplane, and in the service of her country."

Mrs. Fort was asked to submit an itemized statement of the funeral expenses to the Ferry Command in Long Beach, but there was no reimbursement from the military. The family did receive a $250 Civil Service death benefit.

The WAFS were nervous at first that adverse publicity—the death of a young American woman—might jeopardize the program. That never happened. What's more, their commitment to the program was unchanged. "It is remarkable," said an internal ATC history, "that this first fatality among so small a group of women pilots, all bound together by ties of friendship and a common interest in flying, had no serious effects on the morale of the WAFS. There is no indication that the death of Cornelia Fort caused any resignations from the organization or any reluctance to carry on with the ferrying missions assigned."

In fact, three weeks after her death, four women took part in a mission that was seen as a tribute to Cornelia and a chance to prove just what the WAFS were made of. Betty Gillies, Nancy Batson, and two other WAFS had a mission to take four PT-26s, which were PT-19s with closed cockpits, from Hagerstown to Calgary, Alberta. Betty, as leader, took them at dawn from Hagerstown to Joliet, Illinois, the first day. By the time they found a boardinghouse and a restaurant for supper, it was ten o'clock. At 4 A.M., Betty had them up again, and they flew that day to

North Platte, Nebraska. The third day they made it to Great Falls, Montana. They had traveled 700, 600, and 850 miles in planes that averaged 100 miles an hour—when they weren't on the ground during fuel stops. The next day they landed in Calgary. They had made the trip in record time. They and the entire WAFS were commended by Colonel Baker for their work.

Still, there were repercussions in the Army Air Force. The Ferrying Command ordered that WAFS were no longer to fly on missions with men, even in separate planes. Other new rules included one that women could not fly from a day before their menstrual periods until two days after. Nancy Love appealed to common sense, and within a month all the new orders had been rescinded; women were at last allowed to advance as far as their abilities would take them.

Not long after the funeral, Aubrey Blackburne, Cornelia's old instructor, received a letter from Nancy Love. "She said she felt she owed it to me to tell me that the military investigation following the midair collision completely exonerated Cornelia of any blame in any way," Aubrey said. "She also said, 'If it'll be of any consolation, Cornelia was at least unconscious, if not dead, from the collision, because she was too good a pilot not to have cut the switch and turned off the gas before crashing.' And I agreed with her because Cornelia—she wasn't afraid. If the last thing she was conscious of was that she was going in, she still was absolutely not afraid."

Twenty-one

Since her first lesson, about 1,100 days earlier, Cornelia had spent 1,103 hours and 25 minutes aloft. For all the time Cornelia and Aubrey shared in the air and in talking about flying, though, she had never spoken to him about the magic she felt, about the exhilaration, the sense of liberation.

"She was concerned about being an excellent pilot," he said. "She devoted her whole soul and energy and thoughts and money to become an excellent pilot, and she accomplished her desires."

But Cornelia, in her letters and in her articles, set out to describe the spiritual joy she got from flying. If there is a valedictory, it is surely in the letter Cornelia wrote to her mother on January 28, 1942, a little more than a year before she was killed. As she prepared to leave Honolulu, knowing full well she might meet death at any time, she poured out her heart. For all the peril she had faced, for all the tears and struggle she had been through, it was joy and life that filled her:

> I want you to know that except for not seeing you in the last weeks when I've ached for you so, my life has been exceedingly happy. Thanks to the environment, both physical and spiritual, that you and Dad gave me, my life has been rich and full of meaning.
>
> I've loved the green pastures and the cities, the sunshine on the plains, and the rain in the mountains. Springtime in New York and fog in San Francisco.

Books and music have been deeply personal things to me, possessions of the soul. I've loved the multitudinous friends in many places and their many kindnesses to me. I've loved the steak and red wine and dancing in smoky night-clubs, self-important headwaiters who bring the reams of French bread and wine sauces in New Orleans. I've loved the ice coldness of the air in the Canadian Laurentians, the camaraderie of skiing, and the first scotch and soda as you sit in front of the fire.

I loved my blue jeans and the great dignity of life on the ranches. I loved foxhunting even with its snobbishness, I loved the deep pervading tiredness after six hours of timber-topping.

I dearly loved the airports, little and big. I loved the sky and the planes, and yet, best of all, I loved flying. For it too was a deeply personal possession of the soul. I loved Johnny [Koons], because he knew what I meant when we were flying and I suddenly grinned or clapped my hands because the inside excitement was too great not to grin.

I loved it best perhaps because it taught me utter self-sufficiency, the ability to remove myself beyond the keep of anyone at all—and in so doing it taught me what was of value and what was not.

It taught me a way of life—in the spiritual sense. It taught me to cherish dignity and integrity and to understand the importance of love and laughter.

For I have loved many people and many places and many things, and best of all I have loved life, and especially American life. And if I can say one thing in truth, it is that to

my friends and my convictions I have brought all the loyalty
and integrity of which I was capable.

If I die violently, who can say it was "before my time"?
I should have dearly loved to have had a husband and
children. My talents in that line would have been pretty
good, but if that is not to be, I want no one to grieve for me.

I was happiest in the sky—at dawn when the quietness
of the air was like a caress, when the noon sun beat down,
and at dusk when the sky was drenched with the fading light.
Think of me there and remember me, I hope, as I shall you.

With love,

Cornelia

Epilogue

ornelia and the other WAFS opened the door for 1,100 women who graduated from Jackie Cochran's training school and flew during World War II as WASPS, Women's Airforce Service Pilots. The WAFS were in fact folded into the WASPS in 1943. The program, though, did not last through the war. As victory grew closer in Europe, more and more male flyers returned to the States. Concurrently, flight instructors were being released from training schools. Both wanted the ferrying jobs the women had undertaken. The men found sympathetic ears in Congress, and the WASPS were disbanded without thanks or ceremony on December 20, 1944. Betty Gillies and others wrote to the Pentagon, offering to stay on for a dollar a year, but they were no longer welcome in the military. "It broke my heart," said Teresa James, who tried unsuccessfully to join the Chinese Air Force before taking over one of her parents' flower shops. "I just wanted to fly." There had been no military status, and there were no benefits. When the women sought jobs with the airlines after the war, they were offered stewardess positions. It was not until 1977, after a long campaign, that they were granted retroactive military status and benefits.

A private airport in East Nashville, not far from where Fortland stood, is named for Cornelia.

Acknowledgments and Notes

*D*aughter of the Air owes its existence to the Fort family and its willingness to share memories, scrapbooks, letters, personal effects, and, above all, time. I am indebted particularly to Chloe Frierson Fort, Dr. Dudley Fort Jr., Leontine Linton LaPointe, and the late Rufus Fort.

The following are due special thanks as well:

- The WAFS and WASPS. I have made a number of friends among both services, and I consider it a great blessing to have been able to meet and talk with them. This is an extraordinary group of women from a grossly overlooked portion of our history.
- Sarah Lawrence College, especially its archivist, Patti Owen, who helped unlock what was a real turning point in Cornelia's life, and Priscilla Hawkins.
- Bruce Dobie of the *Nashville Scene,* for whom I initially wrote the piece that became this book.
- John Bridges, for his editing work on the *Scene* piece, and on this book, and for coming up with the title, which I think is terrific.
- Debby Bowen, for the many times she read and criticized the manuscript, and my friend William L. Brooks, for his support and feedback and for a terrific editing pass at one point.
- Morgan Entrekin, who saw the *Scene* piece and called and offered me a book deal. That phone call stands as one of my life's highlights.

- Joan Bingham, for whose editing skills and patience I am extremely grateful, and Natira McDermott and Amy Hundley.
- Lynn Franklin, my agent, whose professionalism, negotiating skills, and shoulder are all appreciated, and Candace Rondeaux.
- Dawn Letson, Nancy Marshall Durr, and Mary Caldera, with the WASP collection of Texas Woman's University.
- Leann Barron, for support and help, and Nikki Mitchell, for being the inspiration she is.
- Richard Matheson and Fr. William Presley.
- And those whose friendship has meant so much through this and so many other times—J. Michael Dolan, Barbara Yontz, Bobbie Beasley, Ron Stone, and Frank Donnelly.

Scores of people contributed time, energy, and artifacts to this book. They are listed in the credits that follow, and I offer each of them my heartfelt thanks. Many were patient through long interviews and repeated follow-ups, and some looked over drafts at various points to help assure me that I'd gotten details and time sequences right. Any remaining errors are mine, not theirs.

I have tried to be painstaking in assembling and checking the details of events that happened more than half a century ago. I weighed plausibility, circumstantial evidence, the nature and consistency of reports, and overall reliability as best I could, trying to sift from often-conflicting interviews and written accounts the most truthful narrative possible. There were a number of episodes, varying from Cornelia's collegiate visits to men's schools to Dr. Fort's insistence that his boys never fly, for which I had conflicting information. I have used phrases like "a family story " when an event described by some was contradicted or simply not remembered by others.

Cornelia herself was not always consistent in her accounts. She told and retold the Pearl Harbor story, for instance, and there were variations in the details. There has been longstanding confusion even about the kind of plane Cornelia and her student were flying at Pearl Harbor. Aubrey Blackburne and Betty Rye Caldwell both remember Cornelia telling them she had gone up in a yellow J-3 Cub. Betty Guild Blake, who flew with Cornelia in Honolulu, says that is impossible, since the only J-3 Cub owned by Ole Andrew was blue and yellow. She also says the Interstate Cadet was used most often for training flights. In addition, Cornelia's logbook records that she was indeed in a Cadet. The details of how she brought the plane in for a landing vary somewhat as well. The number of bullet holes in her plane varies in different versions. A later news story said there were two. Betty Guild Blake, who was there, said there were many.

In a very few cases—as in her flight check at New Castle—I reconstructed Cornelia's experiences after learning what other WAFS had gone through.

I must mention particularly the story of Cornelia's death. There have been many books written about the WAFS, individually and collectively, and those that discuss Cornelia's death invariably say she was killed by horseplay—a male pilot was buzzing her, trying to show off or scare her, and his plane hit hers. There are those who argued passionately, fifty-five years after the fact, that Cornelia had indeed been the victim of such horseplay, which was far from unknown among female pilots. Many had experienced it. Most, though, described incorrectly the way the planes collided. I am convinced that a rumor based on antics the WAFS knew to be common gained quick circulation and credence. Some of those I interviewed, though, were equally convinced it was simply a matter of inattention: Someone drifted too close. My interviews with three of the pilots on that last flight, with on-the-ground eyewitnesses, and with the man who investigated the accident convinced me the last explanation is true. I consider it a sad commentary on my profession that, despite all the books and articles mentioning Cornelia's death, I was apparently the first writer to interview these people. "I've been waiting over fifty years for this call," one of the pilots told me.

If I needed reminding of the importance of arriving at the truth, it came home to me at the end of one of my long conversations with Aubrey Blackburne, who taught Cornelia to fly. More than half a century later, his affection for her was touching.

"If you can shed light on what happened to the child," he said, "well, I'd appreciate it. It's a crying shame that woman had to get killed."

Sources and Bibliography

Cornelia Fort and Other Women Aviators

INTERVIEWS

Betty Rye Caldwell, Chloe Fort, Dudley Fort, Dudley Fort Jr., Rufus Fort, Louise Fort Hardeson (interview conducted in 1980 by Doris Tanner), Charles Kinle, David and Elizabeth Craig Proctor.

JOURNALS AND DOCUMENTS

The personal effects of Cornelia Fort, including diary, logbook, orders, scrapbook, manuscripts, letters, licenses, wallet, and assorted memorabilia.

Carol Kaplan and Mary Glenn Hearne, the Nashville Room, Ben West Public Library, Nashville.

Tanner, Doris Brinker. "Cornelia Fort: A WASP in World War II," *Tennessee Historical Quarterly*, Winter 1981, Spring 1982.

Tennessee Blue Book 1995–96. Secretary of State, Nashville, Tennessee.

BOOKS

Becker, Beril. *Dreams and Realities of the Conquest of the Skies*. New York: Atheneum Publishers, 1967.

Caidin, Martin. *Barnstorming: The Great Years of Stunt Flying*. New York: Duell, Sloan & Pearce, 1965.

Christy, Joe. *The Piper Classics*. Blue Ridge Summit, Pa.: Tab Books, 1988.

Harrison, James P. *Mastering the Sky: A History of Aviation from Ancient Times to the Present*. New York: Sarpedon, 1996.

Hildreth, C. H., and Bernard C. Nalty. *1001 Questions Answered about Aviation History*. New York: Dodd, Mead & Co., 1969.

History of the Air Transport Command: Women Pilots in the Air Transport Command, Historical Branch, Intelligence and Security Division, Headquarters, Air Transport Command, 1946 (declassified in accordance with DOD DIR 5200.10).

Langewiesche, Wolfgang. *Stick and Rudder.* New York: McGraw-Hill, 1944.

Lomax, Judy. *Women of the Air.* New York: Dodd, Mead & Co., 1987.

Nevin, David. *The Pathfinders.* Alexandria, Va.: Time-Life Books, 1980.

Rosenbaum, Robert A., ed. *Best Book of True Aviation Stories.* Garden City, N.Y.: Doubleday & Co., 1967.

Smith, Elizabeth Simpson. *Breakthrough: Women in Aviation.* New York: Walker & Co., 1981.

Stott, Carole. *Into the Unknown.* New York: Hampstead Press, 1989.

Women Pilots in the Air Transport Command: October 1942–1944, Headquarters, Air Transport Command, Statistical Control Division, March 1945 (declassified DOD DIR 5200.9).

Childhood and Family History

INTERVIEWS

Epperson Bond Jr., Combs Fort, Margaret Greenlee, Roupen Gulbenk, Carroll Cole Howell, Morton B. Howell, Mrs. Fabian (Helen Dixon) Kunzelmann, Mrs. Pierce Roberts, David Hugh Thompson.

JOURNALS AND DOCUMENTS

Boston Daily Record, August 27, 1940.

Nashville Banner, June 1, 1970.

Nashville Tennessean, March 23, 1940; June 2, 1970.

Tennessee Market Bulletin, Tennessee Department of Agriculture, June 1952.

Ward-Belmont Hyphen, 1950.

BOOKS

Crabb, Alfred Leland. *Nashville: Personality of a City.* Indianapolis and New York: Bobbs-Merrill Co., 1960.

Creighton, Wilbur F. *Building of Nashville.* Privately printed, 1969.

Doyle, Don H. *Nashville in the New South: 1880–1930.* Knoxville: University of Tennessee Press, 1985.

———. *Nashville Since the Nineteen Twenties.* Knoxville: The University of Tennessee Press, 1985.

Egerton, John. *Nashville: The Faces of Two Centuries 1789–1980*. Nashville: PlusMedia, 1979.

Elliott, Lizzie. *Early History of Nashville*. Nashville Public Library, 1963 reprint.

Ellis, John Joseph. "Belle Meade: Development of a Southern Upper-Class Suburb, 1905–1938." Master of Arts thesis. Nashville: Vanderbilt University, December 1983.

Fort, Homer T., Jr., and Drucilla Stovall Jones. *A Family Called Fort: The Descendants of Elias Fort of Virginia*. Midland, Tex.: Texas Printing Company, 1970.

Fort, Lizzie A. "Genealogy of the Fort Family of Tennessee," unpublished.

————. Historical piece prepared for Fort Family Reunion, July 14, 1927.

Fort, Rufus E. "A Gala Day in the History of Robertson County, Tennessee." Springfield, Tenn.: Record Publishing Co., John W. Judd, ed., May 28, 1884.

Kreyling, Christine, Wesley Paine, Charles W. Warterfield Jr., and Susan Ford Wiltshire. *Classical Nashville: Athens of the South*. Nashville: Vanderbilt University Press, 1996.

National Cooperative Soil Survey. *Soil Survey of Davidson County, Tennessee*, 1977. U.S. Department of Agriculture Soil Conservation Service, in cooperation with the University of Tennessee Agricultural Experiment Station.

Norman, Jack, Sr. *The Nashville I Knew*. Nashville: Rutledge Hill Press, 1984.

Reid, Yolanda G., and Rick S. Gregory. *Home of the World's Finest: Robertson County, Tennessee*. Paducah, Ky: Turner Publishing Co., 1996.

Reynolds, Morgan C. *Seventy Years of Belle Meade Country Club, 1901–1971*. Nashville: Belle Meade Country Club, 1971.

Roster of Soldiers from North Carolina in the American Revolution. Baltimore: Genealogical Publishing Company, 1967.

Stamper, Powell. *The National Life Story: A History of the National Life and Accident Insurance Company of Nashville, Tennessee*. New York: Appleton-Century-Crofts, 1968.

Waller, William, ed. *Nashville, 1900 to 1910*. Nashville: Vanderbilt University Press, 1972.

Wardin, Albert W., Jr. *Belmont Mansion: The Home of Joseph and Adelicia Acklen*. Nashville: Belmont Mansion Association, 1981.

Winters, Ralph L. *Historical Sketches of Adams, Robertson County, Tennessee, and Port Royal, Montgomery County, Tennessee, from 1779 to 1968*. Privately printed, 1968.

Woolridge, J., ed. *History of Nashville, Tenn*. Nashville: Publishing House of the Methodist Episcopal Church, 1890.

Zibart, Carl F. *Yesterday's Nashville*. Miami, Fla.: E. A. Seemann Publishing, 1976.

With help from Belmont University Library; Bill Colbert, Cornelia Fort Airpark; Herbert Fox; Jim Hoobler, Tennessee State Museum; Leland Johnson; Linda Renshaw; Ray Sims, soil scientist, USDA; Sons of Confederate Veterans; United Daughters of the Confederacy.

Teen Years Through College

INTERVIEWS
Tillman Cavert Jr., Mrs. Joel (Mary Sue Vaughn) Cheek, O'Neal Clayton, Mrs. Luellen Granberry Cornelius, Mrs. Peyton (Betty Williams) Evans, Mrs. S. McPheeters (Bobbie Leake) Glasgow Jr., Sally Lowengart Lilienthal, Sarah Goodpasture Little, Alex Pirtle, Mrs. Robbie Shackleford, Mrs. Harrison Shull, Carolyn Gray Trabue.

JOURNALS AND DOCUMENTS
The Campus, 1937–38, 1938–39. Sarah Lawrence College yearbooks.
Nashville Banner, December 28 and 30, 1938.
Nashville Tennessean, December 30, 1938.
New York Times, July 25, 1979.
Esther Raushenbush Library, Sarah Lawrence College.
Sarah Lawrence College, catalogs and student records.

BOOKS
Fattal, Laura. "A Glorious Age: Female Education at the Ogontz School." Catalog and exhibition. The Pennsylvania Historical & Museum Commission and The Pennsylvania State University Ogontz campus, June 1987.

Hobbs, Jack A., and Robert L. Duncan. *Arts In Civilisation*. London: Bloomsbury Books, 1991.

Warren, Constance. *A New Design for Women's Education*. New York: Frederick A. Stokes Co., 1940.

With help from Martha Barnes; JoAnne Barry, archivist, the Philadelphia Orchestra; Janet Denton; Mary Driscoll; Johnnie Fields, Emma's; Diane Fusilli; Shirley Griffin; Barbara Hammond; Christy Matasick, Cheekwood Botanical Gardens; Donna Raymer; Susan Saunders and Jane R. Thomas, Belmont University; Terrie Smith, Abington-Ogontz Campus, The Pennsylvania State University.

Early Flying and Colorado

INTERVIEWS

J. Aubrey Blackburne, Willie Horstman, Lloyd Lair, Vance Pinkerton, Peter Robertson.

JOURNALS AND DOCUMENTS

Colorado State University Library and Archives

Cooper, Gov. Prentice. Diaries, 1939, 1940, Tennessee State Library and Archives.

Fort Collins Coloradoan, Fort Collins, Colorado, Library/Museum.

Blackburne, Aubrey. Remarks at the dedication of Cornelia Fort Airpark, *Denver Post,* March 23, 1943.

Fort, Cornelia. "Lady-Bird," Sarah Lawrence *Alumnae Newsletter,* October 1941.

BOOKS

Fort, Dudley, Jr. "My Aunt Cornelia," unpublished manuscript.

Hansen, James E., II. *Democracy's College in the Centennial State: A History of Colorado State University*. Fort Collins, Col.: Colorado State University, 1977.

With help from Dr. James E. Hansen II; Joanna Holiday; Lillian Lair; Kathleen Lewis at *The Coloradoan;* Reba Massey; Christy Matasick, Cheekwood Botanical Gardens; Jane Matson; Mike McDonald; Jack Miller; Wayne Moore, archivist, Tennessee State Library and Archives; Maria Myshatyn; John Newman; David Presley; Gifford "Ben" Preston; Diane Joy Rutter-Wassom; Barbara Yontz.

Hawaii

INTERVIEWS

Betty Guild Blake, Hazel Stamper Hohn, Dorothy Kelsey, Pat Orcutt, Marty Vitousek, Bud Weisbrod, Art Wildern, Elmore Williams.

JOURNALS AND DOCUMENTS

Air Force Historical Research Agency, Maxwell AFB, Alabama.

Allen, Thomas B. "Return To Pearl Harbor." *National Geographic,* vol. 180, no. 6 (December 1991).

Arakaki, Leatrice R., and John R. Kuborn. *December 1941: The Air Force Story.* Hickam Air Force Base, Hawaii: Pacific Air Forces Office of History, 1991. U.S. Government Printing Office, Washington, D.C.

Fort, Cornelia. "At the Twilight's Last Gleaming," *Woman's Home Companion,* June 1943. Original title, "Ladybirds." (February 7, 1943).

Nashville Banner, March 3, 1942.

With help from Rob Carey; Don F. Eyres; Dan Hagedorn, Reference Team Leader, Archives Division, Smithsonian Institution National Air and Space Museum, Washington, D.C.; Bob Heisner; Honolulu Chamber of Commerce; Priscilla Messner; Butch Patterson.

Home from Honolulu

INTERVIEWS

Hank Hillin, Admiral Desmond Piers.

JOURNALS AND DOCUMENTS

Cornell Daily Sun, May 15 and 16, 1942.

Evening Star, Washington, D.C., March 4, 1942.

Halifax Chronicle, August 9, 1942.

Halifax Herald, August 9, 1942.

Honolulu Advertiser, June 9, 1942.

Junior League Magazine, May 1942.

Leonhirth, Janene. "Tennessee's Experiment: Women as Military Flight Instructors," *Tennessee Historical Quarterly.*

Memphis Commercial-Appeal, June 20, 1942.

Nashville Banner, March 3 and May 8, 1942; March 23, 1943.

Nashville Tennessean, March 19 and July 27, 1942.

New York World-Telegram, May 14, 1942.

Our Shield, publication of the National Life and Accident Insurance Company, March 29, 1943.

San Francisco Call-Bulletin, March 1942.

San Francisco Examiner, March 4, 1942.

Syracuse Herald-Journal, May 18, 1942.

Syracuse Post-Standard, May 18, 1942.

With help from Mark Rose, National Weather Service, and Noel Risnychok, National Climatic Data Center.

Delaware

INTERVIEWS

Bernice Batten, Nancy Batson Crews, Phyllis Burchfield Fulton, Betty Gillies, Teresa James, B.J. Erickson London, Adela Scharr, Barbara Poole Shoemaker, Florene Miller Watson.

Interview, Adela Scharr, September 18, 1980 (conducted by Doris Tanner).

Interview, Nancy Love, part of the series "Men of the Land, Sea & Air," WMAL and Blue Network, September 23, 1942.

Journals and Documents

Associated Press photo caption, transmitted September 10, 1942.

Carter, Rowland. "The Ladies Join the Air Forces," *Flying,* December 1942.

Gillies, Betty. Personal diary, 1942, 1943.

Maltin, Leonard. *Movie and Video Guide 1995*. New York: Signet Books, 1994.

Nashville Tennessean, September 11 and 24, 1942; December 28, 1942; December 28, 1943; December 27, 1945; January 4, 1946; September 12, 1976.

New York Times Magazine, September 27, 1942.

Philadelphia Inquirer, September 11, 1942.

Taylor, Hazel. Reports and letters. Air Force Historical Research Agency, Maxwell AFB, Alabama.

Time, September 21 and 28, 1942.

"WAF Delivers Plane to Post," Fourth Ferrying Group newsletter, Nashville, Tenn., November 5, 1942.

WASP Archive, Texas Woman's University, Denton, Texas.

Wilmington Journal, September 11, 1942.

BOOKS AND FILMS

Books on the WAFS, the WASPS, and their era vary widely in quality and reliability. The best is generally acknowledged to be Marianne Verges's *On Silver Wings,* although it is by no means the most detailed.

Bartels, Diane Ruth Armour. *Sharpie: The Life Story of Evelyn Sharp, Nebraska's Aviatrix.* Lincoln, Neb.: Dageforde Publishing, 1996.

Bohn, Delphine. "Catch a Shooting Star," unpublished book-length manuscript, Woman's Collection, Texas Woman's University, Denton, Texas.

Churchill, Jan. *On Wings to War: Teresa James, Aviator.* Manhattan, Kan.: Sunflower University Press, 1992.

Cole, Jean Hascall. *Women Pilots of World War II.* Salt Lake City: University of Utah Press, 1992.

Granger, Byrd Howell. *On Final Approach: The Women Airforce Service Pilots of W.W. II.* Scottsdale, Ariz.: Falconer Publishing Co., 1991.

Keil, Sally Van Wagenen. *Those Wonderful Women In Their Flying Machines: The Unkown Heroines of World War II.* New York: Four Directions Press, 1990.

Ladies Courageous. Film, 1944. Loretta Young, Geraldine Fitzgerald, Diana Barrymore. Directed by John Rawlins.

Matz, Onas P. *History of the 2nd Ferrying Group*. Seattle: Modet Enterprises, 1993.

Scharr, Adela Riek. *Sisters in the Sky*. St. Louis: Patrice Press, 1986.

Verges, Marianne. *On Silver Wings*. New York: Ballantine Books, 1991.

We Were WASP. Film, 1990. Women Airforce Service Pilots, WWII, Inc.

Women of Courage: The Story of the Women Pilots of World War II. Film. KM Productions, Lakewood, Col.

Zeinert, Karen. *Those Incredible Women of World War II*. Brookfield, Conn.: Millbrook Press, 1994.

With help from Capt. Derek Kaufman, public affairs officer, headquarters, Air Force Recruiting Office; National Climatic Data Center, Asheville, N.C.; Major Joseph Piek, Dept. of the Army; Lt. Col. Greg Smith, Air Force Public Affairs Office, Chicago, Ill.

Long Beach

INTERVIEWS

Louis A. Biggio, Bruce B. Calkins, John C. Irving, Betty Joe Seymour, Warren L. Sparks, Randy Stamme.

JOURNALS AND DOCUMENTS

Nashville Banner, March 23, 1943.

Nashville Tennessean, March 24, 1943.

"Report of Aircraft Accident on Civilian Pilot Cornelia C. Fort, April 6, 1943," Air Transport Command, Army Air Force.

With help from Mary Cannon of Emma's, Samuel Dunlap, Mary Ebert, Ginnie Morgan, Bob Simbeck, Kathleen Simbeck, Lori Street-Tubert, Karleen Vitrano.

Index

Fort, Mrs. Louise Clark, 14, 19, 22, 33, 36, 43, 57, 58, 60, 67, 77–78, 98, 106, 107, 118, 121, 129–130, 140, 158, 162, 167, 195, 196, 199, 202, 204, 219; acceptance in Nashville, 15–16; charitable and social activities, 17–18, 20, 97; Cornelia's concern for, 65, 89, 97, 197, 203; Cornelia's death and, 230–234; courtship and marriage, 15; Dr. Fort's death and, 65; gardens of, 13–15, 17, 20, 21

Fort, Moses, 24

Fort, Pearl, 58, 179

Fort, Dr. Rufus Elijah, 46, 47, 49, 52, 53, 54, 62, 97, 98, 105, 197, 198, 233, 236; and flying, 9–12, 64; and Fortland, 14–15; death of, 65; drinking and, 17, 69; early career, 7–8, 13; illness of, 58–59, 62; relationship with children, 18–20, 25–26, 36, 39–43; rigidity, 33, 37, 122, 135

Fort, Rufus, Jr., 8, 12, 19, 34, 36, 39, 58, 59, 103, 106, 110, 174, 179, 195, 196, 232

Fort, Sallie, 24

Fort Benning, Georgia, 233

Fort Collins, Colorado, 1, 77, 78, 79, 80, 85

Fort Infirmary, 7, 17

Fortland, 13–15, 33, 59, 65, 99, 140, 195, 219; burning of, 196–200, 203, 204, 205

Fourth Ferrying Group, 167

France, 24, 70, 78, 123, 133

Fulton, Dorothy, 194

Geismar, Maxwell, 45, 47, 51, 52, 53, 59–60

George, General Harold, 125, 130, 131–132, 148, 169–170, 172

Germany, 53, 54, 55, 70, 76, 78, 114, 122

Getts, Clark H., 117

Gillette, Ruth, 123

Gillies, Betty, 128, 131–134, 138–139, 141–142, 151, 157, 162–166, 171–173, 175–176, 179, 186–187, 190, 194, 200–202, 203–204, 205, 210, 221, 234, 239

Gillies, Bud, 132, 165, 171, 187, 201

Girls' Cotillion Club, 59

Goodman, Benny, 59, 84

Graham, Martha, 40, 49

Grand Ole Opry, 34

Greenville, South Carolina, 179, 200

Grumman, 171, 187, 201

Guild, Betty, 91, 93–96, 101–102, 225

Hagerstown, Maryland, 156, 201, 206, 234

Halifax *Herald,* 118

Hampton Field, 68

Harper's Bazaar, 183